Welcome

US Army Aviation in 2025

Vietnam was the world's first helicopter war. The US Army may not have been the first military service to use helicopters in combat, but it used them in Vietnam in a revolutionary way. Never had so many helicopters been used in combat and with such ambition.

As a result, a whole new jargon entered the military lexicon. Soon all the world knew 'Air Cav' as the 1st Air Cavalry Division was known. They landed their helicopters in 'hot LZs' or landing zones under enemy fire. When casualties needed to be evacuated from a jungle clearing the Air Cav called for a 'dust off'. US soldiers flew into battle across Vietnam on the Bell UH-1 Iroquois, but all the GI's called it the 'Huey', after its original HU-1 designation. Artillery pieces and supplies were flown across rivers and mountain ranges by the Boeing Vertol CH-47 Chinook, nicknamed 'Big Windy' because of the huge downdraft from its twin rotors.

The spirit of the Air Cav pioneers lives on in today's US Army aviators. While the US Army still fields more than 4,000 helicopters, as well 250 fixed wing aircraft and hundreds of drones, making it the world's fourth biggest air arm, it continues its pioneering aviation spirit by adopting new types of aerial weapons. The US Army now operates more unmanned aerial vehicles/systems (UAV/UASs) or drones, to give them their popular name, than the USAF. American army aviators fly their own fleet of

LEFT: Vietnam was the first 'helicopter war' thanks to the US Army investment in air mobility. (US ARMY)

LEFT: Tim Ripley in Kandahar, Afghanistan. (TIM RIPLEY)

ultra-modern spy planes to monitor deep behind enemy lines and US Army Special Operations Force pilots have an unmatched record of pulling off daring missions in combat zones around the world.

In *US Army Aviation in 2025* we tell the story of the military aviators from the early pioneering days in the 1960s through to the battlefields of the 21st Century. We look at the main army aviation units and describe their helicopters, aircraft and drones.

We then look ahead at the new generation of weapon systems being brought into service to fight future wars. Although US Army aviation is synonymous with Vietnam, it now operates a wide range of aerial weapons that are moving it beyond the helicopter. The US Army has long recognised that warfare's third dimension – air – is essential for victory on the ground, but that does not mean success in the air has to be delivered by rotorcraft. The US Army is always looking for new ways to win in the air, as well as on the ground.

Tim Ripley
Editor
July 2025

BELOW: Air assault the US Army way. (US ARMY)

Contents

US Army Aviation

The UH-60 Black Hawk is the US Army's most numerous helicopter. (US ARMY)

Every US Army combat aviation brigade has its own company of armed MQ-1C Gray Eagle UAVs. (GENERAL ATOMICS)

AH-64 Apaches and OH-58 Kiowa Warriors collaborated in scout-attack teams to find and destroy enemy armour. (US ARMY)

Fixed wing surveillance aircraft have long been used by the US Army to monitor crisis zones around the world. (US ARMY)

The mighty CH-47 Chinook has been the US Army's primary heavy lift helicopter since the 1960s. (US ARMY)

The Army National Guard has a fleet of 212 UH-72 Lakota utility helicopters for homeland security and emergency response. (US ARMY)

ISBN: 978 1 83632 116 3
Editor: Tim Ripley
Data and photo research: Joseph Ripley
Senior editor, specials: Roger Mortimer
Email: roger.mortimer@keypublishing.com
Cover Design: Steve Donovan
Design: SJmagic DESIGN SERVICES, India
Advertising Sales Manager: Sam Clark
Email: sam.clark@keypublishing.com
Tel: 01780 755131
Advertising Production: Becky Antoniades
Email: Rebecca.antoniades@keypublishing.com

SUBSCRIPTION/MAIL ORDER
Key Publishing Ltd, PO Box 300, Stamford, Lincs, PE9 1NA
Tel: 01780 480404
Subscriptions email: subs@keypublishing.com
Mail Order email: orders@keypublishing.com
Website: www.keypublishing.com/shop

PUBLISHING
Group CEO: Adrian Cox
Publisher: Steve O'Hara

Published by
Key Publishing Ltd, PO Box 100, Stamford, Lincs, PE9 1XQ

Tel: 01780 755131
Website: www.keypublishing.com

PRINTING
Precision Colour Printing Ltd, Haldane, Halesfield 1, Telford, Shropshire. TF7 4QQ

DISTRIBUTION
Seymour Distribution Ltd, 2 Poultry Avenue, London, EC1A 9PU

Enquiries Line: 02074 294000.

Ready to Meet Tomorrow's Challenges Today

US Army Aviation in 2025

ABOVE: The AH-64E Apache provides the strike power of US Army Aviation. (US ARMY)

BELOW: Bell's V-280 is forming the basis of the future long-range assault aircraft. (US ARMY)

According to its head, Major General Clair Gill, US Army Aviation must be able to fight tonight, while at the same time keeping ahead of rapid technological developments. Speaking to the annual Mission Solution symposium at Fort Novosel in Alabama in January 2025, Gill laid out his roadmap for the future.

According to the US Army Training and Doctrine Command (TRADOC), he said that US Army Aviation must prepare to defeat an enemy that is evolving at the rapid pace of technology and also maintain the readiness to be able to "fight and win tonight. We have to have a sense of urgency and purpose about our collective readiness. We have to adapt to the challenges of the future, while we are tethered to the reality of the here and now."

Gill said the branch has been here before: "We've seen belligerent nations and non-state actors. We've weathered changing administrations and inconsistent funding. And we've pushed through recruiting challenges as the economy has ebbed and flowed. So we find ourselves in another interwar period. Once again, our army is in transition – transformation, in fact. We have clear guidance from our leadership to enhance warfighting readiness, deliver combat-ready formations, transform at scale/pace and continue to foster our profession of arms as the army shifts its focus to large-scale combat operations".

Key topics at the symposium included the changing nature of modern warfare, such as drones, human-machine integration, additive manufacturing, machine learning, autonomous systems, artificial intelligence-enabled maintenance conditions, resilient networks,

Major General Clair Gill

Major General Clair Gill. (US ARMY)

Gill is the commander of the Aviation Center of Excellence at Fort Rucker (Fort Novosel between April 2023 and June 2025) in Alabama. He was commissioned into the US Army Aviation Branch from West Point in 1994. In 2000, he commanded the 'Blackwidows' Assault Helicopter Company of the 9th Battalion, 101st Aviation Regiment. He then served three years on the Joint Reconnaissance Task Force of Joint Special Operations Command. In 2012, Gill returned to the 101st Airborne Division, where he commanded 4th Battalion (Assault), 101st Aviation Regiment, for three years. He deployed with his battalion to Forward Operating Base Shank in Afghanistan in 2014, supporting combat operations throughout Regional Command – East. In 2016, he was promoted and commanded the 10th Combat Aviation Brigade, simultaneously deploying the unit to Iraq, Afghanistan, Kuwait, Korea and Europe. He completed a Senior Service College fellowship at the Central Intelligence Agency in 2016 and is a Master Army Aviator with 3,400 flight hours in his logbook.

rotorcraft with an open architecture and modularity.

According to Gill: "Our 'Big Five' is rapidly being fielded across the entirety of our army right now. The future long-range assault aircraft is bringing a generational leap forward in distance and speed that we haven't seen in our lifetime. Army aviation is the proponent for integrating unmanned aerial vehicles/systems (UAV/S) at every echelon, while also serving as the trail boss for synchronising airspace management in a complex operating environment."

Dependence on legacy systems cannot be neglected though: "We will always fight with what we have. Not only must our industry partners provide the technology for the future, they also must ensure that our legacy systems are sustained and can keep pace to fight and win today."

Gill said the leaders at the event shared the same passion "for how we leverage the talent that emulates from training right here on Fort Novosel, and graduates to our warfighting formations to create war-winning advantage for our army and the joint force." In his update about the state of the branch, Gill covered topics including flight school, unit aircrew experience, aviation and transformation, unmanned

BELOW: The Army National Guard provides aviation support for local authorities across the US in times of natural disasters and other emergencies. (US ARMY)

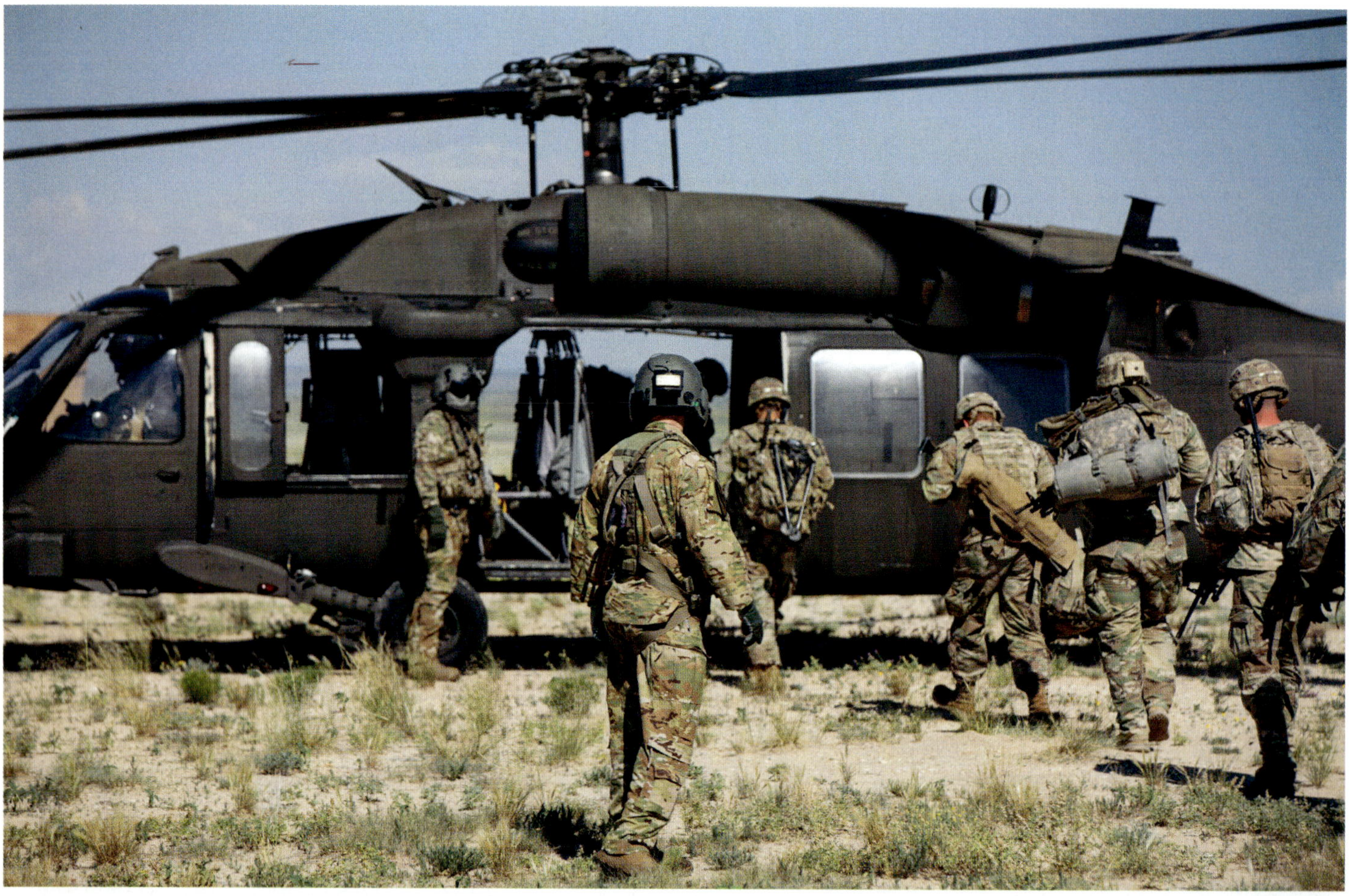

ABOVE: Ever since the Vietnam conflict, the US Army has invested heavily in helicopters to carry out air assault missions to land troops behind enemy lines. (US ARMY)

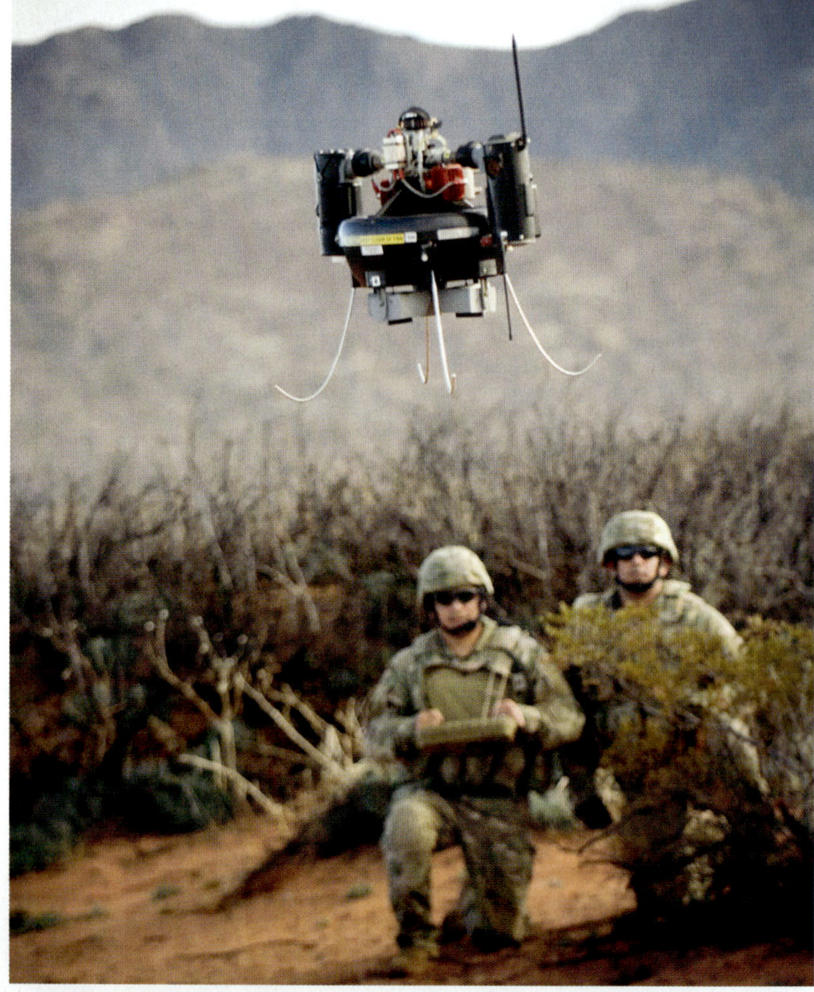

aviation, airspace, safety trends, professional military discourse and aviation warfighter culture.

General Gary M Brito, commander of TRADOC, spoke about his organisation's ongoing efforts to help brigade commanders in the field to build warfighting readiness as they continue to focus on transformation: "Aviation has always been extremely relevant. I sense it's going to be even more relevant as we transition and maintain overmatch in large-scale combat operations and multi-domain operations. Fires, sensor to shooter, support to casualty evacuation, delivery of our troops, long-range fires... you name it. That's no different than what we've done before, but it speaks to the relevance as we transform the types of aircraft and the way we train."

This includes adapting Basic Combat Training and Advanced Individual Training, to ensure that US Army aviators are learning what they need in the future, which includes understanding what it means to be a member of a cohesive team and squad.

As to the speed of institutional transformation to accommodate commanders' warfighting readiness, Brito said it's not perfect, but it will enable commanders to train their forces and meet the warfighting demands that the Chief of Staff of the US Army has laid out in his priorities.

RIGHT: The US Army is now leading the way in developing UAVs in response to the rapid development of AI and robot technology. (US ARMY)

US Army Aviation

US Army Aviation is one of the core branches of the US Army, on a par with the infantry, armour, artillery and engineers. It has the stated mission of "finding, fixing and destroying any enemy through fire and manoeuvre and to provide combat support and combat service support in co-ordinated operations as an integral member of the combined arms team".

US Army helicopters, fixed wing aircraft and unmanned aerial vehicles (UAVs) are assigned work in aviation battalions, regiments and combat aviation brigades (CABs), which in turn are placed under the command of US Army divisions and other formations. US Army aviators also fly and maintain the reconnaissance aircraft owned by US Army Intelligence and Security Command.

Units are spread across the active-duty force, as well as components from the Army National Guard (ARNG) and US Army Reserve (USAR). The ARNG and USAR are trained and equipped to the same standards as their active duty comrades and, over the past 25 years, have been regularly mobilised to deploy to active combat zones as part of what was dubbed the 'global war on terrorism'. Reserve aviators have pulled duty in Afghanistan, Iraq, Syria and elsewhere around the Middle East. Reserve component combat aviation brigade headquarters have also routinely had active duty units placed under their command.

As a service branch, US Army Aviation is responsible for the training of personnel, development of tactical doctrine and the procurement of new equipment. The head of the branch, Major General Clair Gill, is its "tribal chief", who makes sure the case for army aviation is heard in the corridors of power in the Pentagon and is responsible for ensuring that the aviation branch fits into the way the US Army wants to fight.

Currently, the US Army boasts a fleet of more than 4,250 helicopters, fixed wing aircraft and UAVs.

US Army Aviation Inventory, April 2025

	Number in Service	On Order
Attack Helicopters		
AH-64E Apache	647	31
AH-64D Apache	98	
Transport Helicopters		
CH-47F Bk I	465	
CH-47F Bk II	16	
HH/ UH-60M Blackhawk	166	48
UH-64 L/V	921	
Training/Utility		
UH-72A/B Lakota	478	
Fixed Wing Aircraft - Transport/Utility/Training		
C-12F	95	
C-12J (Beech 1900)	3	
C-12U	11	
UC-35A (Citation Encore	27	
C-20H (Gulfsream IV)	1	
C-26 Metroliner	11	
Cessna 208	1	

	Number in Service	On Order
Grob 120TP	6	
T-4D	4	
Dash-8	1	
Fixed Wing Aircraft - Surveillance/SIGINT		
MC-12S EMARSS	23	
RC-12X	19	
EO-5	3	
Global Express	1	2
Unmanned Aerial Vehicles		
General Atomics MQ-1C Gray Eagle	202	12
Special Operations Force Helicopters/Aircraft		
MH-60	72	
MH-47G Chinook	51	10
AH/MH-6	47	
C-27J	7	
C-212	5	
UV-20 Porter	1	

FAR LEFT: The CH-47 Chinook is the mainstay of US Army heavy lift power. (US ARMY)

LEFT: A fleet of more than 200 fixed wing aircraft are operated by the US Army in surveillance, transport and utility roles. (US ARMY)

The Wings of America's Army

The origins of US Army Aviation

the battle, alerting the general to the Confederate threat, allowing reinforcements to be sent to turn the tide. The famous French military advisor to the Union Army, Count de Joinville praised Lowe's intervention, saying: "You, sir, have saved the day!"

After Orville and Wilbur Wright made the first controlled, sustained flight of an engine-powered, heavier-than-air aircraft with the Wright Flyer on December 17, 1903, the US Army moved to exploit the potential of these new 'aircraft'. The Aeronautical Division of the US Army's Signal Corps was formed in August 1907 and, seven years later, it was renamed the Aviation Section.

American military pilots took their biplanes to France in 1917 after the US entered World War One, dogfighting German pilots over the Western Front. A period of rapid expansion followed as the potential of air power was recognised in Washington DC. Between 1918 and 1926, the US Army Air Service experimented with new types of aircraft and tactics. Airpower advocates, led by Billy Mitchell, saw aircraft as war-winning weapons and pushed for the US to form an independent air arm like the British Royal Air Force (RAF).

The compromise was the establishing of the US Army Air Corps, which controlled all

ABOVE: Balloon pioneer Thaddeus Lowe helped turn the tide for the Union Army in the Civil War Battle of Seven Pines in 1862. (US DOD)

America's first use of aircraft to influence combat can be dated back to May 1862 when the Balloon Corps of the Union Army helped defeat Confederate forces during fighting around Richmond, Virginia.

From a balloon basket over the battlefield, the intrepid aerial pioneer Thaddeus SC Lowe observed rebel troops moving to trap a contingent of General George McClellan's army. Lowe used a telephone in his basket to relay messages to McClellan's headquarters at a crucial point in

RIGHT: The US Army Air Service confronted the German air force over the trenches of the Western Front in World War One. (BOSTON PUBLIC LIBRARY, PRINT DEPARTMENT)

land-based US airpower until June 1941. On the eve of the US entry into World War Two its name was changed to the US Army Air Force (USAAF). Although nominally under the control of the US Army, it was increasingly independent and oversaw the development of a massive fleet of strategic heavy bombers, which were ultimately armed with atomic bombs. In September 1947, the US Air Force (USAF) was inaugurated as a separate service.

At this point, the US Army lost almost all of its aircraft, except for a small contingent of Taylorcraft L-2 Grasshopper observation planes used to spot targets for artillery units and flying senior officers around battle zones. All other US military aviation was split between the USAF, US Navy and US Marine Corps. In 1948, the Key West Agreement formalised this set-up and limited the US Army's air power to tactical reconnaissance and medical evacuation roles.

The expansion in the use of helicopters during the Korean War, prompted the Key West Agreement to be revisited and the US Army was allowed to operate helicopters up to 5,000lb in weight for troop transport and battlefield combat missions. As rotocraft technology advanced, the weight limited was revised, which opened the way for the development of the iconic airframes that saw service in Vietnam: the Bell UH-1 Iroquois or 'Huey', Boeing Vertol CH-47 Chinook and Bell AH-1 Cobra.

From 1947 until 1983, US Army aviation assets were controlled by proponent branches based on aircraft and unit type. Cargo helicopters came under the Transportation Corps, while the Infantry Branch looked after assault helicopters and the Armor Branch took on developing attack helicopters. Aerial rocket artillery helicopters came under the Field Artillery Branch, observation/reconnaissance aircraft were the responsibility of the Military Intelligence Branch and aerial medical evacuation units were controlled by the Medical Service Corps. This confusing line of authority was only abolished on April 12, 1983, when the modern-day US Army Aviation Branch was formed.

ABOVE: Observation aircraft such as the Taylorcraft L-2A Grasshopper were the only aircraft to pass into US Army service in 1947 after the USAF became an independent air arm. (ALAN WILSON)

LEFT: The controversial airpower advocate Billy Mitchell led the drive to create an American strategic bomber force that was used to decisive effect in World War Two. This ultimately led to the birth of the USAF in 1947. (USAF)

US Army Helicopters Go to War

From Vietnam to Syria

ABOVE: The AH-1G Cobra was the definitive gunship of the Vietnam conflict and its design set the standard for future attack helicopters. (US ARMY)

Aviation pioneer Igor Sikorsky is credited with designing the first mass produced military helicopter, the Sikorsky R-4. The idea of using rotating blades to generate a 'disc' that could be used to create lift had been around for many years, but Sikorsky was able to turn the concept into a functioning reality.

The Germans had used basic auto-gyros in small numbers during the early years of World War Two, but only a handful ever saw service. Sikorsky flew his prototype R-4 in January 1942 and the US Army Air Force placed their first order he following year. Both the US and British military recognised the battle-winning potential and urged Sikorsky to accelerate testing and production of the R-4. By January 1944, the first R-44s were deployed to Burma, serving with the US contingent fighting the Japanese in the jungles of the Asian country and made history by rescuing the pilot of a downed Allied aircraft.

Helicopter technology moved rapidly after World War Two and all the branches of the US military had operational helicopter units by the start of the Korean War in 1950. They were quickly deployed to help the United Nations forces fight off the Communist invasion. US Army and US Air Force helicopters were used extensively to rescue downed airmen or recover battlefield casualties using the iconic Bell H-13 Sioux. This helicopter with its distinctive glass bubble cockpit was immortalised in the opening sequence of the 1970 film *M*A*S*H*, which revolved

RIGHT: As US troops in Vietnam were withdrawn from 1969, the 101st Airborne Division took on an increasing burden of combat operations. (US ARMY)

Vietnam was the likely venue for the division's first combat deployment.

Although the new division's organisation looked a lot like a conventional infantry division – it had three brigades, eight infantry battalions, an artillery regiment and support units – everything about it was oriented to air mobility. Helicopters were integrated into every unit and tactical procedure used by the division. It had its own aviation group, with three battalions of air assault helicopters that, in theory, could move a whole brigade's worth of troops simultaneously in one lift. A contingent of Boeing Vertol CH-47 Chinook heavy lift helicopters were provided to transport the fuel, ammunition and other supplies to the division's forward operating bases. ➤

LEFT: After the first Battle of la Drang valley, the 1st Cavalry operated across Vietnam until 1971, often deploying rapidly by helicopter when a crisis developed. (ICEMANWCS)

BELOW: Operation Desert Storm in 1991 saw the US Army AH-64A Apache attack helicopter debut in a full-scale shooting war, with devastating effect. (US DOD/COMBAT CAMERA)

army a fictional US Army mobile army surgical hospital during the Korean War.

US involvement in the Vietnam conflict steadily escalated during the first half of 1965 in a bid to roll back advances by Communist forces. By the autumn of that year, the US Army's only air mobile division would be in action in the country's Central Highlands. A handful of US helicopter units had arrived to support US advisors in the early years of the decade as US President John F Kennedy ramped up support for the government of South Vietnam. Communist Viet Cong guerrillas and North Vietnamese regular troops had staged offensives across the south in the early months of 1965, prompting Washington to respond. President Lyndon Johnson ordered US regular troops to South Vietnam to take the fight to the Communists and prevent the fall of the pro-US government in Saigon.

At the end of June 1965, President Johnson approved plans to deploy the first divisional-sized US Army formation to Vietnam: the airmobile division or, as it was officially titled, the 11th Air Assault Division (Test). US Army chiefs felt the division needed a more prestigious title and, on July 1, 1965, it was officially renamed the 1st Cavalry Division (Airmobile) and it inherited that famous unit's traditions and battle honours. All of its subordinate air mobile infantry and reconnaissance units adopted the titles of US Army cavalry units. The move was a big boost for morale and the newly minted cavalrymen soon started to call themselves the 'Air Cav'.

The 11th Division had been set up at Fort Benning in Georgia in February 1963 with the mandate to test and trial using helicopters to fight on future battlefields. It was no secret that

ABOVE: The laser guided Hellfire missiles fired from Apaches devastated the Republican Guard's tank divisions south of Baghdad in March and April 2003. (US DOD/COMBAT CAMERA)

BELOW: The US Army massed hundreds of helicopters in Kuwait in the spring of 2003 ahead of the invasion of Iraq. (US DOD/COMBAT CAMERA)

Airborne firepower, in the shape of armed Bell UH-1 'Huey' helicopters, was integral to everything the division did. Gunships were incorporated into each of the air assault units to fly escort during troop insertion missions. The artillery regiment had its own battalion of rocket armed Hueys to provide fire support when the division was operating beyond the range of traditional tube artillery support. Armed Hueys and Bell OH-13 Sioux scout helicopters were grouped together in the division's reconnaissance battalion, or air

cavalry regiment as it was known. They were the eyes and ears of the division and were tasked with flying over enemy territory to collect intelligence, identify landing zones (LZs) for air assault operations by the air mobile infantry and strike rapidly at any targets that appeared.

Over the next seven years the number and size of helicopter-equipped US Army units surged as a result of a string of battlefield successes, which began with the Battle of la Drang valley in 1965. At the peak of the war, there were two air assault divisions – the 1st

Cavalry Division (Airmobile) and 101st Airborne Division (Air Assault) – in Vietnam. Each had more than 400 helicopters to allow them to manoeuvre across the battlefield. Each US Army line infantry division had its own air assault battalion to allow it to conduct local air mobility operations around their own area of responsibility. There were also scores of independent or corps level units, including reconnaissance, rocket artillery, troop transport and heavy lift, which could be assigned to units for specific operations. New or enhanced helicopters were brought into service to boost the capability of the Air Cav.

After Vietnam, the US Army invested heavily in new rotary wing airframes and developed a concept of operations – AirLand Battle – to integrate helicopters closely with ground units. AirLand Battle called for units, from battalions up to army corps, to penetrate deep into the enemy's rear to surround and eventually destroy their main force. The concept envisaged helicopters being used to lift troops behind enemy lines, to move supplies forward to advancing ground units and to destroy enemy armour with surprise missile attacks. Rough terrain, darkness or severe weather would not provide the enemy with shelter or safe haven because of the widespread use of night vision equipment, advanced radar sensors and electronic surveillance.

By 1990, each US Army division-sized formation had been provided with a combat aviation brigade

with attack helicopters and troop and cargo transport rotorcraft to enable it to put AirLand Battle into practice. Divisions also had a cavalry squadron for reconnaissance, which combined scouts equipped with both armoured vehicles and aircraft. Each corps headquarters was also provided with their own independent aviation brigades, which included two battalions of McDonnell Douglas AH-64A Apache attack helicopters, to give corps commanders the ability to strike deep behind the frontline at enemy second echelon forces. The US Army also had a unique airmobile unit, the 101st Airborne Division (Air Assault), which was trained and equipped to conduct strategic operations far behind enemy lines.

Between August and October 1990, seven aviation brigades and numerous small support units were sent to Saudi Arabia, under the command of the US Army's XVIII Airborne Corps. By the eve of the land phase of Operation Desert Storm on February 24, 1991, the US Army had deployed a massive force of helicopters in the Middle East, including 278 AH-64As, 131 Bell AH-1F/S Cobras, 299 Sikorsky UH-60 Black Hawks, 64 UH-60Vs, 24 EH-60s, 295 Bell OH-58C Kiowas, 92 OH-58D Kiowa Warriors, 314 UH-1s and 127 CH-47s.

Operation Desert Storm was the first combat test of the AH-64A and the AirLand Battle concept. In the aftermath of the war, the US Army heaped praise on the Apache, crediting its AH-64A crews with the destruction of more than 500 tanks, 120 armoured personnel carriers, 30 air defence systems, 120 artillery pieces, 325 other vehicles, 10 radar sites, 50 bunkers, 10 helicopters and other aircraft on the ground. Thanks to the AH-64A video recording systems these claims could be analysed extensively and were generally considered accurate. Overall, the coalition claimed to have destroyed or captured 3,000 Iraqi tanks, so the Apache's contribution to the victory was considerable.

ABOVE: A US Army AH-64A Apache on the prowl over the Iraqi desert. (US DOD/COMBAT CAMERA)

BELOW: US Army UH-60 Black Hawks played a central role in the US occupation of Iraq from 2003 to 2011. (US DOD/COMBAT CAMERA)

The MQ-5A/B Hunter was the first US Army drone to be used in a live conflict and its performance convinced senior officers that they needed to invest more in UAVs. (US ARMY)

Drone Warriors

US Army unmanned aerial vehicles

BELOW: The AAI RQ-7 Shadow has been in US Army service for more than two decades and is being replaced by more modern drones. (US ARMY NATIONAL GUARD, STAFF SGT BRUCE DADDIS)

In the popular media they are called drones, but the US Army defines them as unmanned aircraft systems (UASs) or unmanned aerial vehicles (UAVs). The US Army Signal Corps first experimented using drones as aerial targets in the 1950s and 1960s, but the technology was never mature enough to allow working systems to enter widespread use. It was only in the late 1980s that the US Army got its hands on the first modern drones. The success of Israeli drones during the 1982 Lebanon War prompted the Pentagon to order an experimental batch of Pioneer UAVs from Israel Aircraft Industries (IAI) for use by the US Navy, US Marine Corps and US Army. Eventually, the Pioneers were built in the US by the AAI corporation and dubbed the RQ-2.

The Pioneer was a tactical UAV that took off from a short runway and was able to download live video imagery of the battlefield to a ground control station up to 185 kilometres away. For the time this was a revolutionary capability, and the first US Army Pioneers saw action in the 1991 Gulf War. US Army Military Intelligence initially set up a Pioneer platoon at Fort Huachuca in Arizona and it deployed to Saudi Arabia in the run up to Operation Desert Storm. The UAV platoon flew surveillance and target acquisition missions from King Khalid Military City airfield, close to the Saudi-Kuwait border.

The US Army liked the capabilities of the Pioneer, but soon wanted to buy something better and turned to IAI for the improved Hunter. This was eventually manufactured in the US by TRW and the first RQ-5 Hunters were delivered to A Company, 15th Military Intelligence Battalion (Aerial Exploitation) at Fort Hood in Texas in 1995. The Hunter got its baptism of fire in a live conflict during the 1999 Kosovo war, where the drones were flown from neighbouring Macedonia to look for Yugoslav army tanks and artillery pieces in Serb-controlled province. Unlike the manned fixed wing reconnaissance jets, which had to stay out of Yugoslav anti-aircraft missile and gun envelopes, the Hunter could fly low and was one of the few NATO surveillance systems that could deliver actionable intelligence. Bad weather dramatically hindered high flying reconnaissance aircraft, which added to the importance of the Hunter.

Allied commanders praised the Hunter and its operators for providing some of the best intelligence on Yugoslav military deployments in Kosovo. This came at a cost, with seven being lost. One was even shot down by a machine gunner on a Yugoslav helicopter that flew alongside the drone. However, the losses were considered well worth the valuable intelligence gathered by the Hunter force.

US Army commanders at all levels and in all branches of the service now recognised the potential of drones to transform how the military operated in a range of combat scenarios and plans were drawn up to roll out a range of UAVs. The Hunter was to be upgraded and provide corps-level battlefield surveillance. Brigades would get a new system built by AAI called the RQ-7 Shadow. This was launched from a catapult and could fly out to 109 kilometres. The Shadow entered service in 2002.

After US President George W Bush launched the Global War on Terrorism in response to the 9/11 attacks on the World Trace Center in New York in 2001, the US Army's UAV roadmap was rapidly overtaken by events. In the winter of 2001-2002 US forces invaded Afghanistan and, a year later, 150,000 US troops were gathering in Kuwait ready to begin the attack on Iraq. In March 2003, US tank columns crossed the border and headed for Baghdad. A detachment of Hunters supported the US advance,

backed up by USAF General Atomics MQ-1 Predators.

Once Saddam Hussein's regime collapsed, the US Army settled into occupying Iraq to allow a new pro-US government to be established. Within weeks, insurgents were attacking US troops all around the country and military commanders were demanding overhead surveillance to help give early warning of attacks on their troops and build up intelligence on rebel activity. The US Army Hunter and USAF Predator detachments working in Iraq were soon overwhelmed with calls for help. More drones needed to be deployed as a matter of urgency.

The US Army decided to purchase upgraded Hunters, designated MQ-5B, that were powered with a heavy fuel engine and modified to be able to carry Viper Strike precision munitions. The laser-guided Viper Strike had a small warhead that caused little collateral damage. These second-generation Hunters entered service in late 2005. More than a year later, in

ABOVE: A MQ-1C Gray Eagle is refuelled at a forward operating base in Iraq during the war against the Islamic State in March 2018. (US ARMY, SPC DEVIN FLEMING)

BELOW: The MQ-1C UAV was initially dubbed the Sky Warrior but renamed Gray Eagle in 2010, partly to try to move on from technical problems encountered during the early phase of its development. (US ARMY)

September 2007, a Hunter system recorded its first kill.

Production of the Shadow was accelerated and soon every US Army brigade heading to Iraq had an RQ-7 system, which comprised four air vehicles and two ground control stations. This allowed brigade and battalion commanders to have their own 'eyes in the sky' to monitor local terrain around their bases and fly overwatch on vehicle convoys, giving advance warning of insurgent attacks. By giving every brigade its own Shadow unit, field commanders could deploy them how they wanted and not have to bid to corps and divisional headquarters for drone support. By June 2006, Shadow vehicles had flown a total of 84,000 hours over Iraq and there were an average of seven vehicles in the air over the country 24/7. The RQ-7 was retired in 2024 and a replacement is scheduled to enter service in 2026.

Even this level of drone support was not enough. Now, every infantry squad and platoon requested its own UAVs to monitor insurgent activity at street level. The US Army now wanted several hundred micro- or mini-UAVs, which could be carried in soldier's back packs and manually launched into the air. Each system would cost less than $36,000. They only had a few kilometres range, with the operators being able to watch their video imagery on a tablet computer. These were the ultimate expendable drone.

Several companies were approached to make the handheld drones. The operational need for them was so high that they were often just bought off the shelf and shipped to Iraq or Afghanistan and US troops tested them in the field. If they worked, more were ordered. Systems that didn't were just junked. One of the first mini-drones ordered was the Tactical Mini UAV (TACMAV), which was developed by Applied Research Associates in 2004.

From 2001, the US company AeroVironment produced the Pointer, Raven, Dragon Eye and Wasp drones and several hundred were built over the following decade. In 2012, the US Army placed a $20 million order for the RQ-20A Puma All Environment (AE) hand-launched drone to become its standard mini-drone. More than 1,000 Puma AEs have been built to date.

The US Army was now operating drones on a scale not seen before and it reorganised their management and deployment. In 2003, the US Army Aviation Branch took over responsibility for large tactical drones. – initially the Shadow and Hunter. In 2005, the US Army ordered its own version of the Predator, which was then used by the USAF. It was initially called the Sky Warrior, but was later renamed the General Atomics MQ-1C Gray Eagle. The first test system was deployed to Iraq in 2010 and, over the next decade, every active duty combat aviation brigade received its own MQ-1C company.

Eyes in the Sky

US Army spy planes

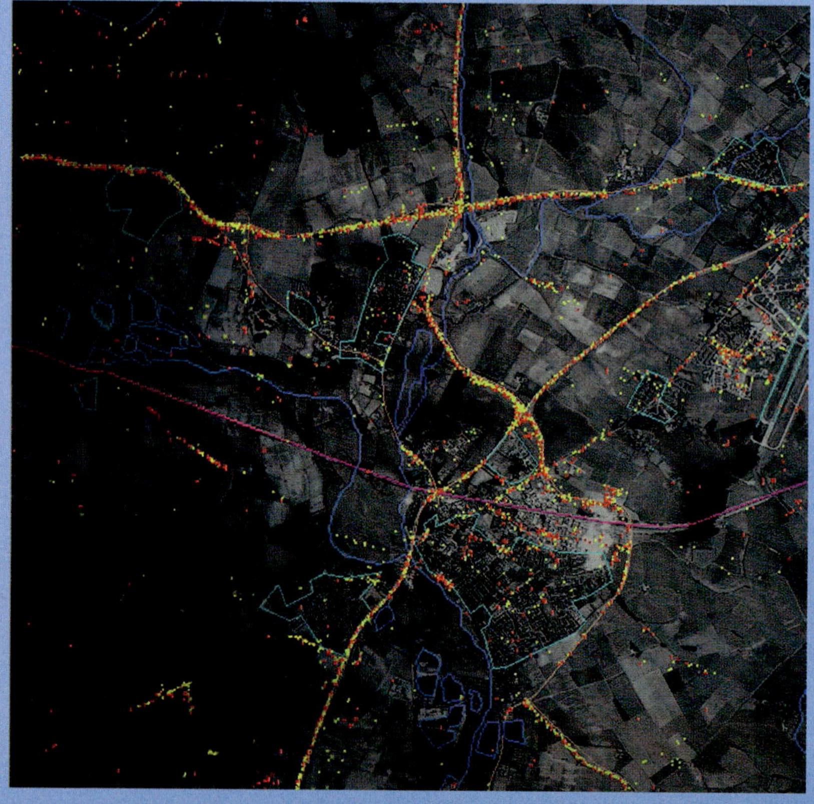

Watching the battlefield from the air has always been an important mission for US Army aviators.

The first American military aviators to see combat belonged to the Union Army's Balloon Corps in the Civil War. In World War One, US Army artillery spotters took to the skies to scrutinise the fall of shot from American gun batteries. This role continued in World War Two, with thousands of Piper L-4 Grasshopper and Stinson L-5 Sentinel light aircraft being purchased to carry artillery spotters. When the USAF was formed in 1947, these artillery spotting aircraft were the only fixed wing aircraft that remained under control of the US Army.

The army ordered a replacement aircraft, the Cessna L-19A Bird Dog, in 1949 and these remained in service until 1974, being renamed the O-1 just before the Vietnam conflict, where pilots provided invaluable support to US soldiers, directing artillery fire and calling in close air support. In

the 1950s, the US Army's Military Intelligence Branch had begun exploring how to exploit new radar technology that could allow enemy tanks, artillery or vehicles hidden in forests or under camouflage to be spotted from the air. This side-looking airborne radar (SLAR) technology could spot large metal objects at night, in bad weather or under foliage. It could also detect when they were moving.

The US Army joined with the US Navy and US Marine Corps to build a bigger observation aircraft in the 1950s, which became known as the Grumman OV-1 Mohawk. It had a distinctive bulbous glass cockpit that was ideal for artillery observers looking at the ground with binoculars. The prototype, YAO-1AF, first flew on April 14, 1959, and the OV-1A entered production in October 1959. Initial versions were destined for visual observation, but the OV-1B featured a pod-mounted early generation SLAR. These aircraft saw active service in Vietnam, helping to find enemy truck convoys hiding under the jungle canopy. This was very basic SLAR technology and, by 1969, a more advanced radar was ready to be installed on the OV-1oD.

After seeing service in later years of the Vietnam conflict, the OV-1Ds were deployed with Military Intelligence (Aerial Exploitation) Battalions in Germany and South Korea to monitor the movement of hostile tank divisions with their SLAR sensors. Several OV-1Ds were

ABOVE: The OV-1C Mohawk was the aerial observation variant of the aircraft, which featured heat sensitive night vision sensors. (US Army)

deployed in combat in the 1991 Gulf War. A number of Mohawks were also converted into electro-intelligence (ELINT) platforms with sensors that could eavesdrop on enemy radio communications, under the designations RV-1C/D.

During the 1980s, rapid advances in radar technology meant the SLAR in the OV-1D was considered obsolete. A new radar technology known as synthetic aperture radar (SAR) was maturing, to allow the collection of three-dimensional radar images of tanks or other vehicles under foliage. The same radar also had a wide area monitoring mode, known as the ground moving target indicator (GMTI), which allowed the live or real-time tracking of enemy vehicles across thousands of square kilometres. This effectively gave US commanders a 'god's-eye view' of a whole theatre of war.

In 1982, the US Army teamed up with the USAF to launch the E-8 Joint Surveillance Target Attack

BELOW: In Vietnam, the Cessna 0-1 Bird Dog was the US Army's primary aerial observation aircraft, helping to direct artillery fire and close air support. (US ARMY)

ABOVE: A USAF/US Army E-8C JSTARS of the 10th Expeditionary Airborne Command and Control Squadron was dispatched to Ramstein Air Base, Germany, in 2021 for NATO exercises. (USAF TECH SGT CHRISTOPHER RUANO)

Radar System (JSTARS) project. This mounted a SAR/MTI radar on a Boeing 707-300 airframe, which allowed the system to be elevated high above the battlefield. Grumman Aerospace (now Northrop Grumman) was awarded the contract to convert the aircraft and install their radars. A revolutionary feature of the JSTARS was a datalink that allowed the radar imagery to be downloaded in real-time to a ground station located in army field headquarters. The USAF provided the aircrew and airframe maintenance, while US Army Military Intelligence analysts were responsible for monitoring the live radar imagery and assessing enemy battlefield manoeuvres.

A prototype E-8 was ready in time to be deployed to the Middle East in 1991 during Operation Desert Storm, to monitor Iraqi tank movements across a huge swathe of Kuwait and southern Iraq. Its crews famously detected the first signs that the Iraqi army was pulling out of Kuwait and helped mobilise a fleet of USAF strike jets to attack troop convoys on what became known as the 'road of death'. Over the next 25 years, the JSTARS saw active service over Bosnia, Kosovo, Iraq, Afghanistan and Ukraine.

Satellite and business jet-based solutions, in effect, rendered the old E-8 too expensive to operate, so by 2020 the JSTARS was slated for retirement and it performed its last operational flight on November 15, 2023. The aircraft had conducted some 14,000 operational sorties, flying more than 141,000 hours over 32 years of service.

RIGHT: USAF and US Army personnel jointly crewed E-8C JSTARS aircraft to allow experts in ground warfare to be on hand to interpret intelligence collected by the aircraft's powerful radar. (USAF)

The arrival of the JSTARS in the early 1990s had led to the retirement of the OV-1Ds from Europe in 1992, from South Korea in September 1996 and, finally, the continental United States in 1996. However, this was not the end of the Military Intelligence Branch's manned fixed wing reconnaissance aircraft. Since the 1970s it had operated a fleet of ELINT aircraft to monitor enemy radio communication traffic under the codename Guardrail. These were initially fitted to Beechcraft U-21 King Air airframes but, in the 1980s, the systems were transitioned to the Beechcraft Super King Air under the designation RC-12. Since then, the RC-12s have seen service around the world helping to eavesdrop on enemy radio communications. Their mission fit has been progressively updated to keep pace with threats, including countering the radio control systems of roadside bombs.

After the war in Afghanistan, the US Army also acquired the USAF's fleet of Beechcraft MC-12W Liberty surveillance aircraft, which boasted electro-optical video cameras, downlinks to stream video off the aircraft and a limited eavesdropping capability. Most of the capabilities of the RC-12 and MC-12W were eventually merged to create the MC-12S Enhanced Medium Altitude Reconnaissance and Surveillance System (EMARSS).

While much of the OV-1D's warfighting role was taken over by JSTARS in the early 1990s, the US Army wanted to retain a limited aerial surveillance capability for use in counter-insurgency and special operations missions. It acquired several de Havilland Dash-7 EO-5/RC-7 airborne reconnaissance low and de Havilland Dash-8 R0-6 airborne reconnaissance low-enhanced aircraft. Over the past 30 years, these aircraft, which are believed to carry power cameras and SAR sensors, have been spotted flying in crisis zones where US covert operations were suspected of being underway. One EO-5 crashed in Columbia in 1999 with the loss of all seven crew during a suspected mission to monitor drug cartel activity.

This decade, the US Army has been moving forward with plans to recapitalise aerial exploitation fleet with new aircraft based on a business jet airframe under the High Accuracy Detection and Exploitation System (HADES) programme. A testbed based on a Bombardier CL-600-2B16 (Series 604) Challenger, dubbed the Airborne Reconnaissance and Targeting Exploitation Multi-Mission Intelligence Systems (ARTEMIS), has been operational in Europe. The Airborne Reconnaissance and Electronic Warfare System (ARES) testbed which utilises a Bombardier Global 6000/6500-class business jet, has been flying trial missions in the Far East.

ABOVE: De Havilland Dash 7 or EO-5/RC-7A short take-off and landing transport was modified under the Airborne Reconnaissance Low programme to carry out surveillance in a variety of non-combat scenarios. (ALAN RADECKI)

BELOW: The Airborne Reconnaissance and Electronic Warfare System (ARES) demonstrator, based on a modified Bombardier Global 6000, helped the US Army develop its next generation of fixed wing surveillance aircraft. (L3HARRIS)

RIGHT: Operations from US Navy warships are routine for aviators of the 169th SOAR (A) to allow them to refuel during long-range missions. Here, an MH-60L lands on the USS *Bataan*. (US NAVY)

BELOW: A pair of MH-47G Chinooks from the 160th SOAR (A) conducting flight deck landing qualifications aboard USS *Hershel 'Woody' Williams* (ESB 4) in June 2021, off the coast of West Africa as part of African Lion 2021. (US NAVY)

In April 2011, a pair of US Army Sikorsky UH-60 Black Hawks modified with stealth features to evade hostile radar tracking flew deep into Pakistan to drop off a team of US Navy SEALs to kill or capture the mastermind of the 9/11 attacks, Osama bin Laden. Operation Neptune Spear, as the mission was codenamed, saw the 160th Special Operations Aviation Regiment (Airborne) (SOAR(A)) deliver the SEAL Team 6 to their target and then safely recover them, all without being detected by Pakistani air defences. It was the most successful US special operations mission this century and confirmed the 'Night Stalkers' as the world's most capable special operations aviation unit.

Owning the Night

Special Operations aviators

Yet only 30 years before, America's Special Operations community had been humiliated by the Desert One debacle when the ad hoc nature of the aviation elements in Operation Eagle Claw was identified as a major weakness that contributed to the failure of the mission to rescue US diplomats from Iran. US Marine Corps pilots had been drafted in to fly US Navy Sikorsky RH-53D Sea Stallion helicopters on the doomed mission. One of the helicopters collided with a USAF Lockheed EC-130 Hercules airlifter, causing the deaths of five servicemen.

The 160th SOAR(A) was formed in the aftermath of that debacle to ensure that US Army Special Operations Forces (SOF) units – the elite Delta Force, US Army Special Forces aka The Green Berets and Rangers – would no longer have to rely on the USAF or US Marine Corps to fly them into action.

Unlike the USAF, which had a long tradition of special operations aviation stretching back to the World War Two air commandos, the 160th SOAR(A) was a new departure for the US Army. A handful of Special Warfare Aviation detachments had been formed in Vietnam, under the umbrella of the 281st Assault Helicopter Company, Airmobile Light, to support the Green Berets. They flew the classic UH-1D 'Huey', but these never rivalled the range and endurance of the big HH-53 'Jolly Green Giant' used by USAF special operations units in southeast Asia.

The intention was to create a unit that supported special operations on a 24/7 basis, so it could rapidly deploy on overseas missions and have a close working relationship with US Army SOF ground elements. Personnel of 160th SOAR(A), dubbed Task Force Brown, are held at high readiness to support the secretive work of the Joint Special Operations Command (JSOC) and its ground elements, Delta Force and SEAL Team 6.

The 160th SOAR(A) was initially formed by transferring companies and sub-units from the 101st Airborne Division (Air Assault) into the new organisation. As the 1980s progressed, the new regiment expanded and developed its own identity after seeing action in Grenada in 1983 and Panama in 1989. The regiment was nicknamed the 'Night Stalkers' because much of its work involved operating under the cover of darkness. Pilots of 160th SOAR(A) pioneered the use of advanced night vision goggles, thermal imaging sensors and terrain following radar in helicopters. During the 1990s and 2000s, the use of this equipment became routine across the rest of the US Army aviation community.

After the formation of 160th SOAR(A), the US Army began several programmes to field dedicated helicopters for its specialist role. The key requirement was to allow the covert delivery of SOF teams behind enemy lines, resulting in the fitting of advanced night vision devices, an air-to-air refuelling capability, secure communications, highly accurate navigation devices and defensive systems to defeat

ABOVE: The US Army Special Operations Aviation Command has its own fleet of CASA-212 tactical transport aircraft, which are used for parachute training and trials work. (US ARMY)

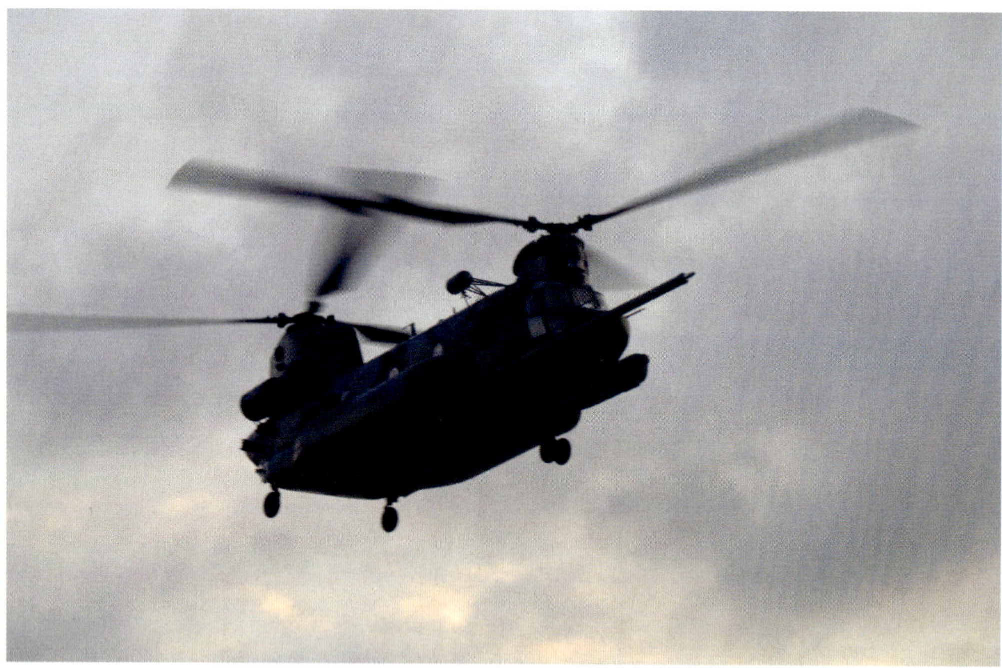

ABOVE: MH-47 Chinooks are used by the 160th SOAR(A) for long-range insertion missions, using air-to-air refuelling to fly deep behind enemy lines. (US AIR FORCE, AIRMAN MATTHEW R LOKEN)

enemy surface-to-air missiles. At first this effort involved the modification of existing UH-60s, Boeing CH-47 Chinooks and Hughes OH-6 Cayuses. These dedicated SOF variants were indicated by an 'M' in their designation – for example, the UH-60 became the MH-60.

In 1987, the formation of the US Special Operations Command (USSOCOM) with full budgetary authority allowed the development of a new generation of SOF helicopters. Although they were developed from existing designs, the advanced MH-60s, MH-47s and MH-6s had their special features incorporated during manufacturing. To support JSOC, the regiment operates unconventional helicopters, including a stealth version of the UH-60 Black Hawk, which made its combat debut in the 2011 raid into Pakistan.

The 160th SOAR(A) underwent its first major test against a well-equipped and determined enemy during the 1991 Gulf War. Its MH-47 Chinooks played a key role in the opening moves of Operation Desert Storm, using their advanced navigation systems to lead a pair of US Army McDonnell Douglas AH-64A Apaches to strike an Iraqi border radar station to open the way for USAF Lockheed F-117 stealth fighters heading to Baghdad for the opening attack of the war. Aviators of the regiment were also heavily involved with inserting covert teams from Delta Force and the US Army Special Forces to carry out sabotage attacks.

Two years later, the 160th SOAR(A) played a key role in the Somalia conflict, which was immortalised in the 2001 movie *Black Hawk Down*. While delivering Delta Force operators and Ranger assault teams, one of its MH-60Ls was shot down and its crew spent several hours surrounded on the ground.

During Operation Enduring Freedom following the 9/11 attacks on the World Trade Center in New York in September 2011, the 160th SOAR(A) was in the forefront of delivering US Army Special Forces into Afghanistan to lead the fight against the Taliban. The long-range

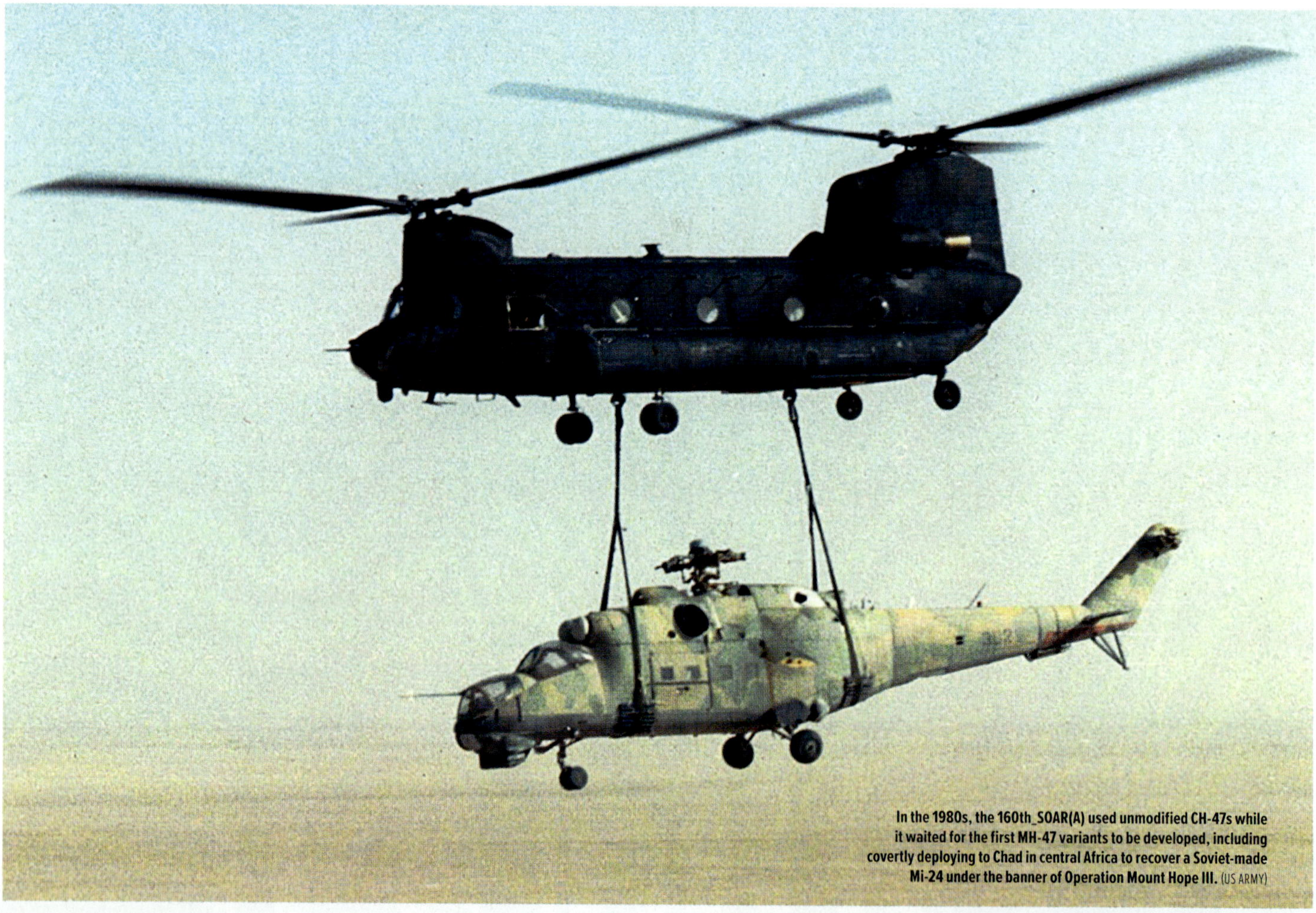

In the 1980s, the 160th_SOAR(A) used unmodified CH-47s while it waited for the first MH-47 variants to be developed, including covertly deploying to Chad in central Africa to recover a Soviet-made Mi-24 under the banner of Operation Mount Hope III. (US ARMY)

MH-60s and MH-47s used their air-to-air refuelling capability to fly over the Hindu Kush mountain range to deliver the first US Army 'boots on the ground' of the Afghan war.

For the subsequent 20 years, the 160th SOAR(A) maintained a continuous presence in Afghanistan to support JSOC and the Central Intelligence Agency in hunting down Taliban and al-Qaeda leaders. Night after night, the MH-47s and MH-60s delivered JSOC assault teams across the country to raid houses being used as hiding places by America's enemies. The 160th SOAR(A) played a similar role during the US invasion of Iraq, carrying JSOC assault teams into action around Baghdad.

JSOC operations in Afghanistan and Iraq made extensive use of USAF General Atomics MQ-1 Predator and MQ-9 Reaper unmanned aerial vehicles (UAVs) to monitor insurgent safe houses and, if necessary, destroy them with bombs or missiles. In 2013, the 160th SOAR(A) received its first MQ-1 Gray Eagle, a version of the Predator modified for use by the US Army. By having its own MQ-1Cs, the 160th SOAR(A) had a dedicated armed UAV capability that was on call when US Army SOF units were committed to operations. In particular, the regiment now had a cadre of MQ-1C operators who were fully qualified and experienced in supporting special operations. They knew all the players in the US JSOC community, so could rapidly deploy on highly secret operations without having to undergo specialist training or mission orientation. The 160th SOAR(A) eventually received two companies of MQ-1Cs, which have seen action in Afghanistan, Iraq, Syria, Somalia and Niger monitoring al-Qaeda and Islamic State.

ABOVE: US Navy SEAL boat teams train with the US Army's 'Night Stalkers' to covertly insert their powerful and heavily armed craft in hostile waters. (US NAVY)

BELOW: The MH-47 has great utility as a parachute dropping platform to deliver US Special Operations Forces behind enemy lines. (US ARMY)

Fighting Force

How US Army Aviation is organised

The key US Army aviation fighting unit is the combat aviation brigade, or CAB, which is the basic aviation component in each fighting division. Since the 1970s, every US Army division has had a strong aviation component that is under its direct command.

The idea is to allow US Army divisional commanders to operate on both the land and in the air in a range of scenarios from full-on conventional combat to counterinsurgency, peacekeeping and humanitarian operations.

Officially, the mission of US Army aviation is to "find, fix and destroy any enemy through fire and manoeuvre" and "to provide combat support and combat service support in co-ordinated operations as an integral member of the combined arms team".

A mix of helicopters and drones are brought together in CABs, to allow divisional commanders to monitor the battlefield in real-time, launch deep strikes against positions far behind enemy lines, to rapidly move troops by helicopters across a range of terrain and to re-supply units by air. By assigning CABs permanently under division command, it enables divisions to routinely think and plan for operations in multi-dimensions. This unity of command allows US Army, divisional, brigade and

BELOW: US Army combat aviation brigades combine helicopters and UAVs into a single fighting formation to achieve maximum impact on the battlefield. (US ARMY, VISUAL INFORMATION SPECIALIST ERICH BACKES)

LEFT: AH-64E Apache helicopters from 1st Battalion, 101st Aviation Regiment, Attack Helicopter Battalion, attached to the 36th Combat Aviation Brigade, during deck qualification training on the USS *Lewis B Puller* in the Arabian Gulf in 2022. (US ARMY, 2ND LT TIFFANY PARUOLO)

LEFT: Soldiers from the 526th Brigade Support Battalion of the 101st Airborne Division (Air Assault) reach up with a sling load loop to a Chinook helicopter at Camp Buehring in Kuwait. (US ARMY, SGT BRANDON HUBBARD)

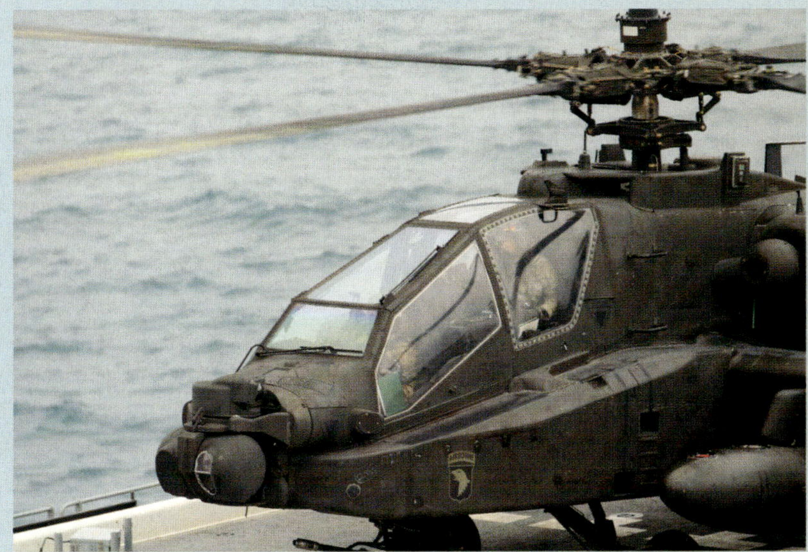

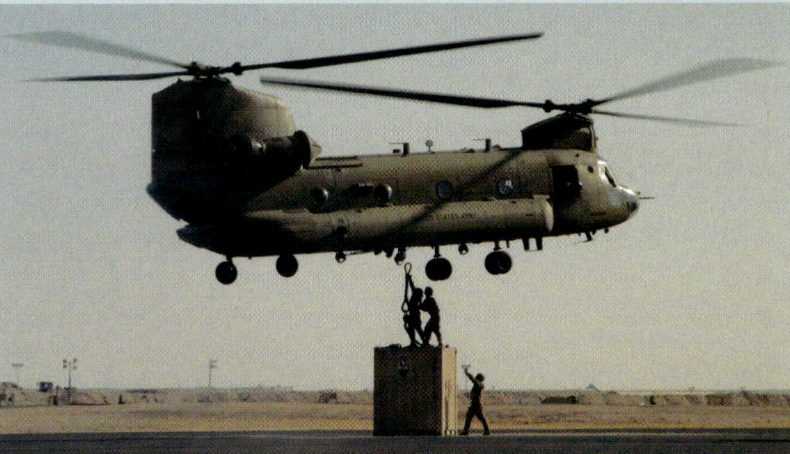

battalion commanders to rely on air support whenever they embark on combat operations.

In its current iteration, US Army CABs are described as "multi-functional brigade-sized units" that are all configured and equipped in the same way. The existing organisation was established 20 years ago to allow a smooth rotation of CABs to combat zones in Iraq and Afghanistan to be undertaken. This standardisation approach ensured that each CAB had a balance of capabilities to meet a range of threats. This ended the previous system, where different types of divisions – armoured, mechanised, light infantry, airborne and air assault – had bespoke aviation brigades attached to them.

The CAB concept is common across regular or active-duty US Army divisions, as well as reserve component aviation units of the Army National Guard and US Army Reserve.

The 11 CABs of the active-duty US Army are configured slightly differently from reserve component CABs, which tend to have older variants of helicopters and do not yet have very many UAVs.

Current active-duty CABs have a combination of Boeing AH-64D or E variant Apache attack/reconnaissance helicopters, Sikorsky UH-60M Blackhawk assault or medium-lift helicopters, Boeing CH-47F

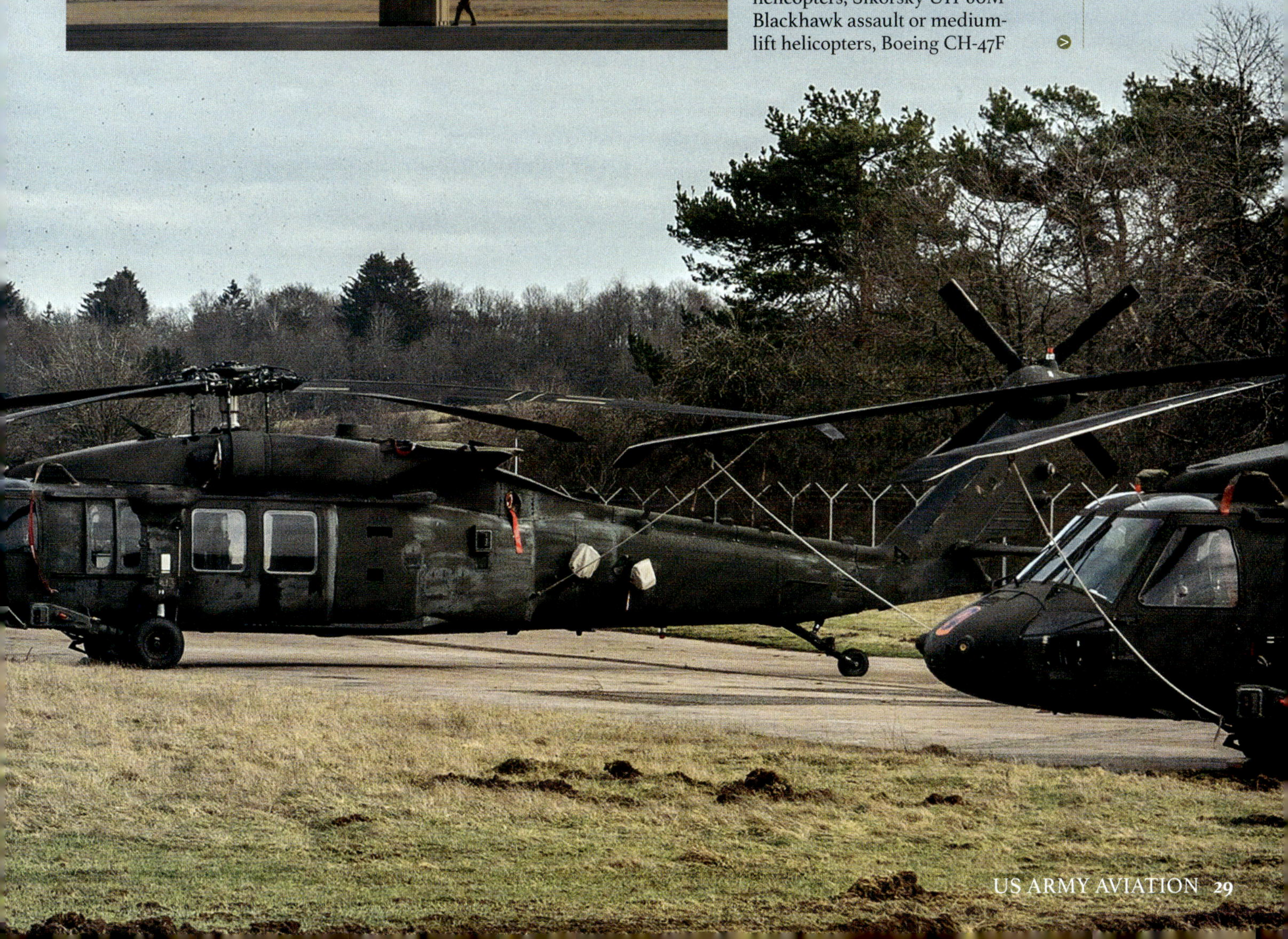

ABOVE: The US Army's attack helicopter units routinely use USAF transport aircraft to move their AH-64s from their home garrisons to overseas battle zones. (US ARMY)

ABOVE RIGHT: An UH-60 Black Hawk modified for snow operations lands on a railway flatcar during a medical training exercise in the Arctic at Fort Wainwright in Alaska. (US NAVY, MASS COMMUNICATION SPECIALIST 1ST CLASS TREY HUTCHESON)

Chinook heavy-lift helicopters and HH-60 medical evacuation helicopters. Each CAB now boasts unmanned aerial vehicles or systems (UAV/UAS) to allow persistent surveillance of the battle space.

In nine of the 11 active-duty CABs, there are two Apache-equipped battalions, each with 24 AH-64s, broken down into three companies of eight helicopters. Two brigades have just one attack/reconnaissance battalion of 24 Apaches. In every division, one of the two Apache units is an air cavalry reconnaissance squadron or battalion. Until the retirement of the RQ-7 UAV fleet in April 2024, air cavalry units combined 24 AH-64s with a company of 12 RQ-7 UAVs to allow the CAB to monitor a screen of terrain in front of their parent division. A replacement for the RQ-7 is expected during 2026. More sustained surveillance of targets deep behind enemy lines is the responsibility of the CAB's organic UAV company, with 12 General Atomics MQ-1C Gray Eagles.

The bulk of the active-duty Apache battalions have been re-equipped with the E model of the AH-64 and the remainder are to convert over the next few years. In a nod to the early days of the 'Air Cav' in Vietnam, several Apache battalions have retained their historic cavalry titles, insignia and regimental traditions, including Stensen hats and horse-mounted parades.

The next most important aviation unit in each CAB is an assault helicopter battalion with 30 UH-60s, which are used to airlift infantry units during air assault operations. The balance of the CAB's helicopters is concentrated in its general support aviation battalion for a variety of

support roles. These include eight UH-60s modified for command-and-control and 15 HH-60M medevac-configured aircraft, as well as 12 CH-47F heavy-lift helicopters to move field guns, bulk supplies or large numbers of troops.

The final element of the CAB is its aviation support battalion, which provides maintenance and other ground support. It includes fuel tankers and other supply vehicles needed to establish forward arming and refuelling points (FARPs) around the battlefield so helicopters can rapidly refuel and rearm to return to the fight.

Each CAB is organised in such a way that it can either fight as a full brigade in major combat operations or be broken down into battalion-sized task forces that can be detached to work alongside each of a division's ground manoeuvre brigades.

Over the past 20 years, US Army CABs have often been detached from their parent divisions to serve six-month or year-long tours of duty in Iraq or Afghanistan during the 'Global War on Terrorism'. During these deployments, CAB headquarters have often taken under command a mix of aviation units from the US Army or allied forces.

In addition to the 11 CABs permanently assigned to US Army divisions, there are two non-divisional assigned CABs that are intended to operate independently or work for corps level headquarters. The 12th Combat Aviation Brigade is based in Europe to support NATO under the command of V Corps. In Washington State, the 16th Combat Aviation Brigade is a reserve formation to support US Indo-Pacific Command. There is an independent aviation task

force assigned to the US 11th Airborne Division in the far north of Alaska, which is trained and equipped for arctic operations.

The US Army has just started an initiative to restructure its CABs to return to a more functional role structure. By the end of the decade, the eight CABs assigned to armoured

and mechanised divisions will become heavy CABs, which will have fewer UH-60s and the light infantry role divisions will have the strength of their air assault units expanded. The 101st Airborne Division (Air Assault) will be provided with an additional battalion of CH-47Fs to allow large air assault operations to be undertaken.

US ARMY COMBAT AVIATION BRIGADE STRUCTURE, 2025

Air Cavalry Reconnaissance Squadron (ACRS)
• 24 × AH-64 Apache

Attack Reconnaissance Battalion (ARB)
• 24 × AH-64 Apache

Assault Helicopter Battalion (AHB)
• 30 × UH-60M Black Hawk

General Support Aviation Battalion (GSAB)
• 8 × UH-60L, 12 × CH-47F Chinook, 15 × HH-60M

Unmanned Aerial System (UAS) Company
• 12 × MQ-1C Grey Hawk UAS

ABOVE: The RQ-7B Shadow UAS was teamed with the AH-64E Apache in air cavalry squadrons attached to each combat aviation brigade, to find targets for the attack helicopters. (US ARMY)

LEFT: MQ-1C Gray Eagle-armed drones are fielded in every active-duty combat aviation brigades to provide long-range and long-endurance strike/surveillance support. (GENERAL ATOMIC)

Find, Fix and Destroy

ABOVE: Missiles in targets. An AH-64E crew of the 16th Combat Aviation Brigade fires an AGM-114 Hellfire missile during a range exercise at the Yakima Training Center in Washington State in 2023. (US ARMY, CAPT KYLE ABRAHAM)

BELOW: Integration of air and land combat systems are central to the way US Army combat aviation brigades fight. (NY ARMY NATIONAL GUARD, SPC HARLEY JELIS)

After inventing the attack helicopter in the 1960s, the US Army has continued to develop battlefield tactics to use these powerful weapons for maximum effect. No other army has as many attack helicopters or uses them in such an aggressive way.

The US Army operates its Boeing AH-64D/E Apaches as battalion-sized units of 24 helicopters, comprising three companies with eight AH-64s. Basic attack/reconnaissance battalions just operate AH-64s and air cavalry reconnaissance squadrons have three Apache troops (companies); until April 2024 a troop of 12 AAI RQ-7 Shadow unmanned aerial vehicles (UAVs) or drones was assigned to these units. Attack helicopter battalions are very flexible combat organisations, which have utility in a range of battlefield scenarios.

The classic US Army attack helicopter mission is known as 'deep strike' against enemy second-echelon forces, such as tanks reserves, command posts, ammunition dumps or lines of communication, hundreds of kilometres behind the front line. These can be either pre-planned strikes against known targets that have already been found by US Army Military Intelligence or sweeps launched to look for targets of opportunity.

Apache battalions are not launched on deep strike missions without extensive preparation of the battlefield, including the detection of enemy anti-aircraft threats, terrain analysis and co-ordination with other parts of the US Army and US Air Force.

Low-flying helicopters are very vulnerable to enemy anti-aircraft guns and surface-to-air missiles, so the attack helicopter commanders plan their routes carefully to avoid those threats and use terrain such as ridges, forests and urban areas to mask them. In large operations, three Apache companies will be assigned to strike their targets from different axis, to complicate the enemy's response.

During deep attacks, AH-64s pilots have to fly fast and low, dodging and weaving past terrain at night using the helicopters' low-level and night-vision systems to stay safe. Battalion and company commanders fly forward during these attacks to monitor progress and adjust the plan if something goes wrong.

When hunting for targets of opportunity, drones are sent ahead

of Apache companies to find enemy positions and confirm the best places to position attacking helicopters.

To try to achieve surprise, the approaching Apaches do not open fire until they all have their target in their sights. Once the AGM-114 missiles start flying and the enemy anti-aircraft guns return fire, Apache crews have to use all their skills to withdraw safely to friendly territory, as well as employing their defensive systems to decoy away enemy surface-to-air missiles and jam enemy radar tracking systems.

When supporting friendly troops defending against enemy tank attacks, Apache battalions can be called forward to engage attacking armour. When enemy armour masses to attack and then breaks cover to move forward, it is very vulnerable to attack from the air. US commanders aim to create 'kill zones' where enemy tank columns can be hit from multiple directions by overwhelming firepower. Once the enemy tank columns enter the kill zone, attack helicopters will be brought forward to engage them. Helicopters will be positioned behind ridge lines, forests and large buildings, before popping up to find targets and let off Hellfire missiles and then drop down behind cover rapidly to avoid detection by enemy anti-aircraft weapons.

To maintain the rate of fire, battalion commanders will rotate their Apache companies throughout the battle, so once a company has gone 'Winchester', or expended all their ammunition, they withdraw and are replaced by a new, fully armed company. The company that is out of ammunition then flies back to the forward arming and

refuelling point (FARP) to rearm, then they will head back into the battle. This battle rhythm ensures the enemy remains under constant missile fire, breaking the back of their attack.

Attack helicopters have an important role to play in what is called the 'close battle', where friendly troops, particularly lightly armed ➤

LEFT: Owning the night – use of advanced night-vision sensors gives US Army aviators a key advantage over their opponents.
(US ARMY, CAPT KYLE ABRAHAM)

BELOW: US Army AH-64E Apache crews are expert at using complex terrain to hide and shield their movements from enemy forces.
(US ARMY, CPL DAVID POLESKI)

infantry, are locked in fire fights with enemy troops. When friendly troops are pinned down by enemy snipers, machine gun positions or dug-in infantry, they can rapidly call up AH-64s to take them out. The sudden appearance of a pair of Apaches is often enough to bring devastating firepower to bear. A well-placed Hellfire can break the back of enemy defences by knocking out key enemy weapons. Saturation fire by 30mm chain guns or Hydra 70 rockets can supress enemy troops, forcing them to dive to the bottom of their trenches, giving friendly troops the chance to advance.

An important US tactic is the use of air assault to deliver troops behind enemy lines to capture important terrain, such as bridges, airfields or strategic enemy positions, and these are heavily dependent on support from attack helicopters. Air assault operations have to be prepared in the same way as deep attack missions, but also involve the movement of dozens of US helicopters carrying hundreds of soldiers. Surprise is a vital ingredient for an air operation to be successful, which places great importance on the role of escorting attack helicopters in case something goes wrong. To achieve surprise, attacks are often undertaken without preparatory artillery or air strikes before air assaults go in. Each air assault company of ten Sikorsky UH-60 Black Hawks are usually escorted by two or four Apaches. They fly just ahead of the

UH-60s and in the seconds before they land, the AH-64s put down supressing firing on the assault troops' objective.

During the approach to the objective, if the assault helicopters come under anti-aircraft fire, some of the AH-64s can peel off to engage the threats to allow the UH-60s to continue safely on their way.

Once the assault troops are safely on the ground, Apaches will fly security patrols around their positions to neutralise any threats until heavy armour and artillery can be brought forward to fully secure the objective from enemy counterattacks.

Over the past 25 years of the 'Global War on Terrorism', US Army attack helicopters have proved indispensable to American counter-insurgency operations. Often, the presence overhead of a pair of heavily armed AH-64s was enough to deter insurgents from attacking US troops. This overwatch role took on many forms.

In Iraq, Afghanistan and Syria, insurgent groups regularly attacked US forward operating bases (FOBs) with rockets, mortars, machine guns or mini-drones. To disrupt these insurgent tactics, Apaches would be sent to patrol around FOBs trying to spot insurgents setting up weapons. The presence overhead of American helicopters would often force the insurgents to call off their attacks.

Overwatch patrols were also routinely flown over US road convoys to try to pre-empt attacks on them with improvised explosive devices (IEDs). Helicopters would fly ahead of the convoys looking for insurgents trying to plant IEDs. The Apaches would engage the bombers and radio warnings to approaching convoys.

A key offensive role in counter-insurgency operations is the launching of raids to kill or capture insurgent commanders or bomb makers. These are in essence small scale air assault operations and are routinely escorted by AH-64s to neutralise any resistance.

The Apache was brought into service in the 1980s to counter massed Soviet tank divisions in central Europe. The 2022 Russian invasion of Ukraine has seen the US Army Aviation Branch look again at its tactics for countering massed tank attacks, with special references to making better use of drones.

ABOVE: The Grafenwoehr Training Area in Germany is used extensively by US Army AH-64E crews to perfect their tactics for hunting enemy tanks. (US ARMY, SGT OMAR JOSEPH, SR)

BELOW: Highly trained and experienced Apache pilots are the US Army's biggest combat advantage. (NATO)

Gunships and Haulers

US Army Aviation in Eastern Europe

RIGHT: Germany-based aviators of the 12th Combat Aviation Brigade routinely deploy across Europe to take part in NATO training exercises. (US NATIONAL GUARD, STAFF SGT CLINTON THOMPSON)

A s the US military ramped up its response to the 2014 Russian occupation of Crimea and growing tension in Eastern Europe, it launched Operation Atlantic Resolve.

This followed more than two decades of steadily running down the US Army presence in Europe, which culminated in April 2013 with the withdrawal of the last M1 Abrams main battle tanks from Germany. At the start of 2014, there were fewer than 30,000 US Army soldiers based in Europe. This included the Germany-based 12th Combat Aviation Brigade (CAB).

To rapidly rebuild the combat capability of the US Army in Europe, the Pentagon ordered a series of rotations of major units to Europe from garrisons in the continental United States. This reduced costs because expensive garrisons and family support infrastructure in Europe were not needed.

Operation Atlantic Resolve called for a small US Army division-sized force, built around an armoured brigade and a combat aviation brigade, to be sustained in Europe, with the major units usually spending nine months at a time in the field. Each rotation involved the brigades moving their main equipment by ship and air, to practise the procedures for reinforcing Europe. A network of camps and ammunition dumps was set up in Poland and elsewhere in Eastern Europe to accommodate the temporarily deployed units. Several pre-positioned equipment storage sites were set around Europe to contain the vehicles and other equipment needed to expand the US Army force to a full-strength division of four brigades in time of crisis or war.

Rotary-wing aviation is integral to the US Army's combat doctrine and, under Operation Atlantic Resolve, a full combat aviation brigade was deployed to Europe for each troop rotation from 2017.

During their deployment time, the elements of CAB were dispersed across Eastern Europe to support individual battalion-sized tasks forces of the armoured brigade. Typically, one aviation task force is usually operating in Romania and Bulgaria, another is working in the Baltic States, and the balance of the CAB operates in Poland. The main CAB headquarters is generally based at Forward Operating Site Powidz, Poland, where administrative logistic support is centred.

The aviation task force is made up of a combination of Boeing AH-64E Apache attack helicopters, Sikorsky UH-60 Black Hawk utility helicopters and Boeing CH-47F Chinook heavy-lift helicopters. This is a flexible structure that allows the rapid reinforcement of additional capabilities for specific missions. By establishing a presence across the length and breadth of Eastern Europe, the CAB is able to swing its helicopters quickly to wherever they are needed. US Army aviation has set up hubs in Estonia, Lithuania, Poland and Romania allowing maintenance and logistic support to be pre-positioned for future contingencies. Therefore, US Army aviation unit has become a common sight around Eastern Europe and allied forces have received experience operating with them.

BELOW: The flight line at the US Army Garrison at Ansbach in Bavaria is home to the 12th Combat Aviation Brigade. (US ARMY, JONATHAN BELL)

Operation Atlantic Resolve
US Army Aviation Rotations, 2015 to 2025

Date	Unit	Helicopters	UAV
Battalion-sized Task Force			
March 2015 to November 2015	Task Force Brawler, 4th Battalion, 3rd Aviation Regiment	AH-64E, UH-60, CH-47F	
November 2015 to August 2016	Task Force Spearhead, 3rd Battalion, 227th Aviation Regiment	AH-64E, UH-60, CH-47F	
August 2016 to March 2017	Task Force Apocalypse, 3rd Battalion, 501st Aviation Regiment	AH-64E, UH-60, CH-47F	
Combat Aviation Brigades			
March 2017 to October 2017	10th Combat Aviation Brigade, 10th Mountain Division	AH-64E, UH-60, CH-47F, HH-60M	RQ-7, MQ-1C
October 2017 to July 2018	1st Air Cavalry Brigade, 1st Cavalry Division	AH-64E, UH-60, CH-47F, HH-60M	RQ-7, MQ-1C
July 2018 to March 2019	4th Combat Aviation Brigade, 4th Infantry Division,	AH-64E, UH-60, CH-47F, HH-60M	RQ-7, MQ-1C
March 2019 to November 2019	1st Combat Aviation Brigade, 1st Infantry Division	AH-64E, UH-60, CH-47F, HH-60M	RQ-7, MQ-1C
November 2019 to July 2020	3rd Combat Aviation Brigade, 3rd Infantry Division	AH-64E, UH-60, CH-47F, HH-60M	RQ-7, MQ-1C
July 2020 to March 2021	101st Combat Aviation Brigade, 101st Airborne Division	AH-64E, UH-60, CH-47F, HH-60M	RQ-7, MQ-1C
March 2021 to December 2021	1st Combat Aviation Brigade, 1st Infantry Division	AH-64E, UH-60, CH-47F, HH-60M	RQ-7, MQ-1C
December 2021 to September 2022	1st Air Cavalry Brigade, 1st Cavalry Division	AH-64E, UH-60, CH-47F, HH-60M	RQ-7, MQ-1C
September 2022 to May 2023	Combat Aviation Brigade, 1st Armored Division	AH-64E, UH-60, CH-47F, HH-60M	RQ-7, MQ-1C
March 2023 to October 2023	3rd Combat Aviation Brigade, 3rd Infantry Division	AH-64E, UH-60, CH-47F, HH-60M	RQ-7, MQ-1C
October 2023 to July 2024	1st Combat Aviation Brigade, 1st Infantry Division	AH-64E, UH-60, CH-47F, HH-60M	RQ-7, MQ-1C
July 2024 to February 2025	1st Air Cavalry Brigade, 1st Cavalry Division	AH-64E, UH-60, CH-47F, HH-60M	MQ-1C
March 2025 to December 2025	Combat Aviation Brigade, 1st Armored Division	AH-64E, UH-60, CH-47F, HH-60M	MQ-1C

FAR LEFT: The CH-47F variant of the iconic Chinook helicopter provides battlefield mobility to US and allied land forces by moving troops, supplies and M777 155mm howitzers. (NATO)

FAR LEFT BELOW: A CH-47F Chinook assigned to the 1st Battalion, 214th General Support Aviation Battalion prepares to lift a UH-60 Black Hawk during a crash recovery training simulation on the Hohenfels Training Area in Bavaria. (US ARMY, PFC CARLOS MARQUEZ)

LEFT: US Army UH-60 Black Hawk medium-lift helicopters provide tactical mobility and specialist support, such as casualty evacuation. (NATO)

THE DESTINATION FOR AVIATION ENTHUSIASTS

KEY Publishing

Visit us today and discover all our publications

Aviation News is renowned for providing the best coverage of every branch of aviation.

Airforces Monthly is devoted to modern military aircraft and their air arms.

and subscribe to your favourite magazine...

/collections/subscriptions

Free 2nd class P&P on BFPO orders. Overseas charges apply.

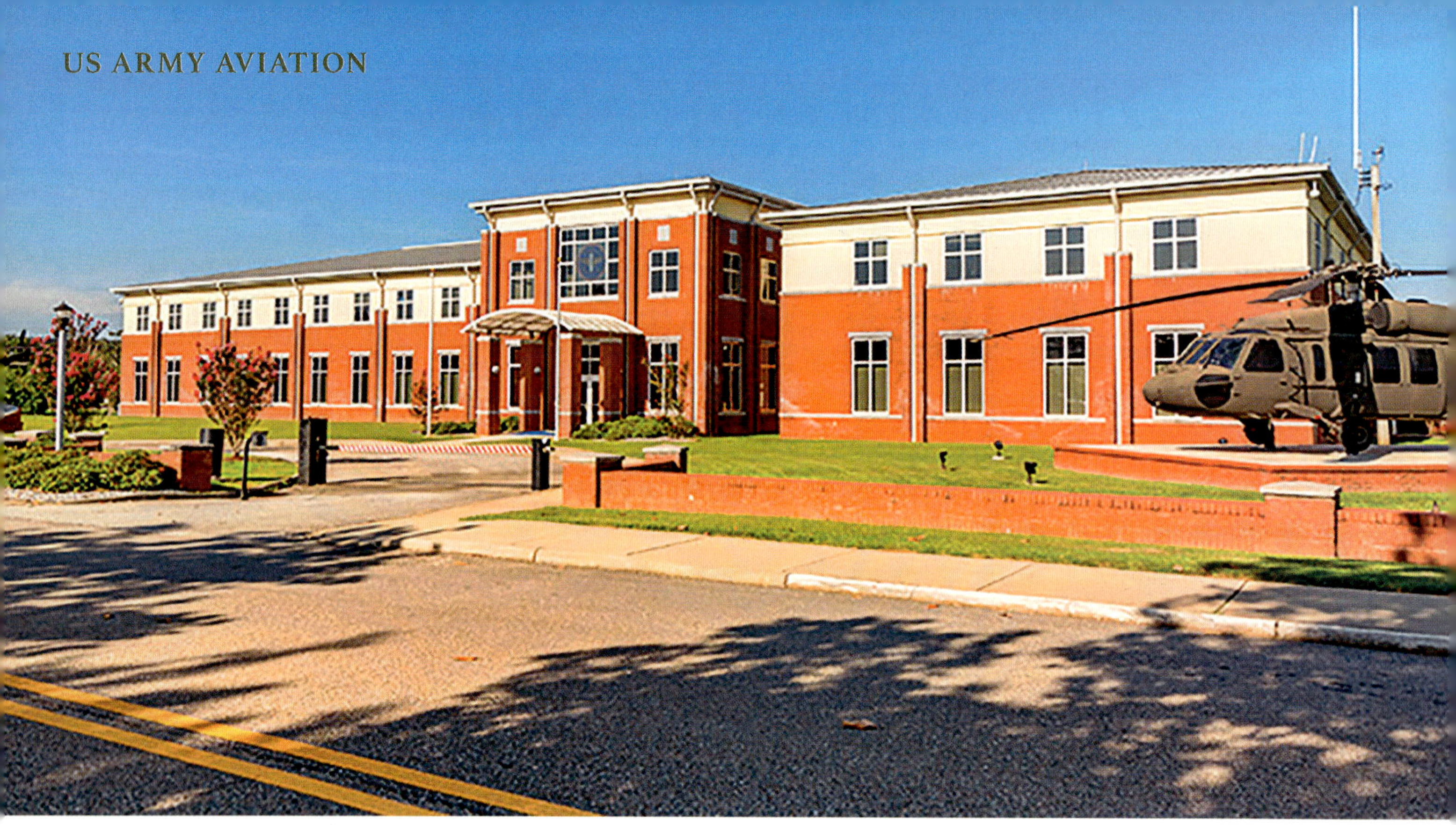

The US Army Aviation Center of Excellence

Building the next generation

ABOVE: The US Army Aviation Center of Excellence at Fort Rucker, Alabama, is the home of the service's aviation branch. (US ARMY)

Fort Rucker in Alabama is the home of the US Army Aviation Branch and has been the sole site for US Army helicopter air and ground crew training since 1973. The training of artillery observation spotters started at what was then Camp Rucker in World War Two and the US Army Aviation School was set up at the post in 1953. Two years later, the camp became Fort Rucker, and the US Army Aviation Center was opened. In 1956, the US Army gained full control over the training of its aircrew and maintenance personnel from the US Air Force, opening the away for the rapid expansion of Fort Rucker.

As part of the drive by the Pentagon to rid the US military of sites named after rebel Confederate officers from the Civil War era, the post was redesignated Fort Novosel in April 2023, in honour of Chief Warrant Officer Michael J Novosel – he won the Medal of Honor in Vietnam for flying his helicopter into hostile fire to rescue troops trapped behind enemy lines. The post was previously named for a Civil War-era officer, Confederate Colonel Edmund Rucker. On the order of Defense Secretary Pete Hegseth, the post was renamed again in June 2025 for Edward Rucker, an aviator in World War One.

RIGHT: A fleet of UH-72A Lakota helicopters are based at Fort Rucker to train the next generation of US Army aviators. (US ARMY)

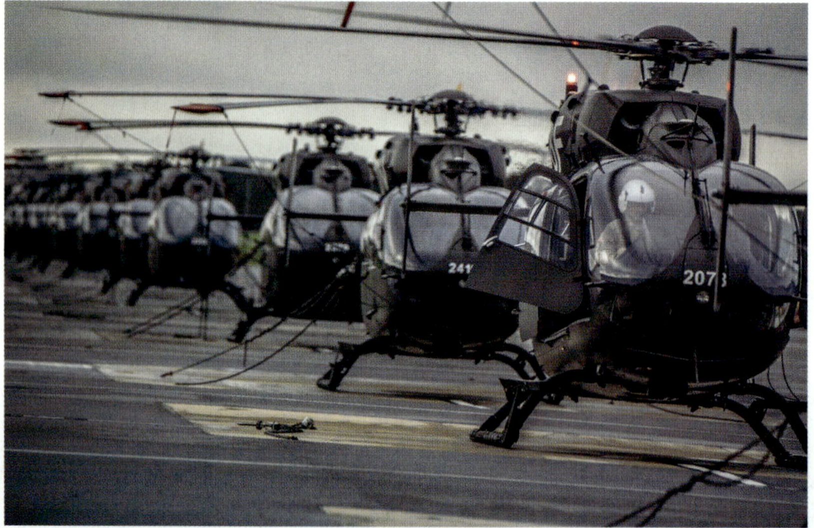

	Location	Helicopters/UAV	Unit Role
Aviation Centre of Excellence	Fort Rucker, Alabama		
1st Aviation Brigade	Fort Rucker, Alabama		
1st Battalion, 13th Aviation Regiment	Fort Rucker, Alabama		Aviation Soldier Training
1st Battalion, 145th Aviation Regiment	Fort Rucker, Alabama		Aviation Officer Training
2nd Battalion, 13th Aviation Regiment	Fort Huachuca, Arizona	MQ-1C	UAV training
110th Aviation Brigade	Fort Rucker, Alabama		
Headquarters and Headquarters Company	Fort Rucker, Alabama		
1st Battalion, 11th Aviation Regiment	Fort Rucker, Alabama		Air Traffic Control
1st Battalion, 14th Aviation Regiment	Hanchey Army Heliport, Alabama	AH-64D/E	AH-64D/E Training
1st Battalion, 212th Aviation Regiment	Lowe Army Heliport and Shell Army Heliport, Alabama	UH-60M/L	UH-60M/L Training
1st Battalion, 223rd Aviation Regiment	Cairns Army Airfield and Knox Army Heliport, Alabama	UH-72, CH-47F	UH-72 & CH-47F Training

Today, most US Army aviation training, of aircrew and ground maintainers, is carried out at Fort Rucker, except for some parts of unmanned aerial vehicle (UAVs) and fixed-wing training that takes place at more suitable locations. Fort Rucker is home to the United States Army Aviation Center of Excellence (USAACE), which is the headquarters of the aviation branch. The commander of the USAACE is also head of the aviation branch. He oversees all US Army aviation training, as well the development of aviation tactical doctrine and has an important role in the development of requirements for new helicopters, aerial weapons and UAVs. USAACE does not oversee the procurement of new helicopters and other aviation systems, which is carried out by the US Army Aviation and Missile Command at Redstone Arsenal in Huntsville, Alabama.

Potential US Army helicopter pilots start their initial training on the Airbus UH-72A Lakota at Fort Rucker before progressing onto conversion training to fly the more advanced combat helicopter types. The 1st Aviation Brigade conducts initial training and the 110th Aviation Brigade carries out flying training at Fort Rucker's five airfields.

Officers and other ranks are trained to be helicopter pilots, with the latter becoming warrant officers. It is an important part of the US Army aviation career structure that long-serving commissioned officers and warrant officers can continue to fly throughout their service to retain their experience and skills in the aviation branch as instructors and specialists.

An important part of the USAACE is to maintain the traditions and history of army aviators, so it is the site of the United States Army Aviation Museum.

LEFT: Billy Croslow, US Army Aviation Center of Excellence command historian, conducts a history session focused on the development of battlefield helicopters with aviation lieutenants at the US Army Aviation Museum during the Basic Officer Leadership Course. This is intended to help aviators gain a sense of how technology and doctrine develop and foster an appreciation of their branch's corporate identity. (US ARMY, KELLY MORRIS)

BELOW: US Army aviators perfect their flying and tactical skills across the large training area at Fort Rucker. (US ARMY, STAFF SGT SCOTT TYNES)

Combat Aviation Brigades

Active duty order of battle

RIGHT: An armament and avionics maintainer with the 1st Air Cavalry prepares to load an AH-64 Apache helicopter's M230 30mm chain gun for gunnery training at an airfield near Grafenwoehr in Germany. (US ARMY, SGT GREGORY T SUMMERS)

1ST AIR CAVALRY COMBAT AVIATION BRIGADE

The brigade is part of the 1st Cavalry Division, which is based at Fort Hood in Texas, and is assigned to the US Army's strategic heavy armoured reserve formation, III Armored Corps.

In a nod to its role as the US Army's first air mobile unit to see action in the Vietnam war in 1965, the brigade retains the Air Cavalry title in its unit name. The 1st Cavalry Division is also one of the US Army's most historic divisions, tracing its roots back to its formation in 1923. Many units within the division have adopted the traditions of US Army cavalry regiments that played a prominent role in the 19th century Indian Wars and Civil War.

During World War Two, the division traded its horses in for tanks and saw service as an armoured division. After its service in the Vietnam war as 'Air Cav', it reverted to the armoured role, which it has held to this day.

The division's aviators took their McDonnell Douglas AH-64A Apaches into action in the 1991 Gulf War. In January 2004, it deployed to Iraq on the first of several deployments during the 'Global War on Terrorism', including playing a leading role in the Battle of Fallujah in October and November 2004. The division's aviators also deployed regularly to Iraq, Afghanistan and Syria over the past 20 years to reinforce other formations.

Since 2017, the brigade has deployed three times to Europe to work with NATO forces as part of Operation Atlantic Resolve.

BELOW: Air Cav in the 21st century. The 1st Air Cavalry Combat Aviation Brigade upholds the traditions of its famous predecessor from the Indian Wars in America's West and the Vietnam war in the 1960s. (US ARMY, DESTINEE RODRIGUEZ)

	Location	Helicopters/Aircraft/UAV	Unit Role
1st Air Cavalry Brigade (1st Cavalry Division)			
Headquarters and Headquarters Company	Fort Hood, Texas		
7th Squadron, 17th Cavalry Regiment "PaleHorse"	Fort Hood, Texas	AH-64E	Air Cavalry Reconaissance Squadron
1st Battalion, 227th Aviation Regiment "Attack"	Fort Hood, Texas	AH-64E	Attack/Reconnaissance Battalion
2nd Battalion, 227th Aviation Regiment "Lobos"	Fort Hood, Texas	UH-60	Assault Battalion
3rd Battalion, 227th Aviation Regiment "SpearHead"	Fort Hood, Texas	UH-60L, HH-60M, CH-47F	General Support Aviation Battalion
F Company, 277th Aviation Regiment "Godfathers"	Fort Hood, Texas	MC-1Q	UAS Company
615th Aviation Support Battalion "Cold Steel"	Fort Hood, Texas		Ground Support Unit

	Location	Helicopters/Aircraft/UAV	Unit Role
Combat Aviation Brigade (1st Armored Division)			
Headquarters and Headquarters Company	Fort Bliss, Texas		
3rd Squadron, 6th Cavalry Regiment "Heavy Cav"	Fort Bliss, Texas	AH-64E	Air Cavalry Reconaissance Squadron
1st Battalion, 501st Aviation Regiment "Iron Dragons"	Fort Bliss, Texas	AH-64E	Attack/Reconnaissance Battalioon
3rd Battalion, 501st Aviation Regiment "Apocalypse"	Fort Bliss, Texas	UH-60	Assault Battalion
2nd Battalion, 501st Aviation Regiment "Iron Knights"	Fort Bliss, Texas	UH-60L, HH-60M, CH-47F	General Support Aviation Battalion
Company E, 501st Aviation Regiment "Executioners"	Fort Bliss, Texas	MC-1Q	UAS Company
127th Aviation Support Battalion "Workhorse"	Fort Bliss, Texas		Ground Support Unit

1AD COMBAT AVIATION BRIGADE

The 1st Armored Division (1AD) traces its history back to 1940 when it was formed weeks after the establishment of the US Army's tank force. It is nicknamed 'Old Ironsides' after the USS *Constitution*, one of the US Navy's original warships, and was the first US armoured division to see battle in World War Two.

The division is currently based at Fort Bliss near El Paso in Texas and is part of the III Armored Corps, providing America's heavy armoured reserve force. It has its own dedicated aviation brigade, nickname 'Iron Eagles', which was first formed in 1986 at Ansbach in Germany, as part of the expansion of US Army aviation in the 1980s.

After seeing action in the 1991 Gulf War, the Germany-based aviation brigade was routinely deployed to the Balkans on peacekeeping missions. From April 2003 to July 2004, the brigade deployed to Iraq in support of Operation Iraqi Freedom.

For five years from 2006, the 1st Armored Division was without its own aviation components after it relocated from Germany to Fort Bliss.

Its aviation brigade was transferred to the 1st Infantry Division as part of a major shake-up of its organisation.

The 1AD's combat aviation brigade was reformed to restore the division's aviation capability in 2011. Just over a year later, units from the brigade began deploying to Afghanistan to augment other units. In 2019, the brigade deployed to Afghanistan to support US and NATO forces in the central Asian country. During its deployment it flew 58,000 combat hours conducting aerial reconnaissance, attack and lift operations.

ABOVE: 1st Armored Division infantry soldiers assume a fighting position after jumping from a UH-60 Black Hawk helicopter during air assault training. (US ARMY, SGT ALEXANDER NEELY)

LEFT: 1AD AH-64 Apache attack helicopters carried out live fire training exercises at Torun in Poland during their deployment to Eastern Europe in 2022. (US ARMY NATIONAL GUARD, SGT JOHN SCHOEBEL)

ABOVE: Heading east, 1st Combat Aviation Brigade AH-64 Apache helicopters prepare for take-off at Chièvres Air Base in Belgium before flying to Poland for NATO exercises. (US ARMY, VISUAL INFORMATION SPECIALIST PIERRE-ETIENNE COURTEJOIE)

RIGHT: Two CH-47F Chinook helicopters proudly sport the 'Big Red One' insignia assigned during the Commemorative Airborne Operation at La Fière, France, June 9, 2019, to commemorate the 75th anniversary of the D-Day landings. (US NAVY, MASS COMMUNICATION SPECIALIST 2ND CLASS ERIC COFFER)

1ST COMBAT AVIATION BRIGADE

The 1st Infantry Division is widely known as 'the Big Red One' after its iconic shoulder patch. It is the oldest continuously serving active-duty division in the US Army and celebrated its centenary in 1917, marking 100 years of continuous service.

During its time in Vietnam in 1960s, the division made extensive use of helicopters, before it returned to its home at Fort Riley in Kansas in 1970. The build-up of US Army aviation capabilities in the 1980s led to the expansion of the division's aviation component, with the formation of its aviation brigade in 1986. At this point it was known as the division's fourth brigade.

The division fought in the 1991 Gulf War and its helicopters played an important role in its battles with Iraqi troops. As a result of a re-organisation of the US Army in the mid-1990s, the division was re-located to Germany. Over the next five years it was heavily involved in peacekeeping missions in the Balkans and its aviation brigade deployed as a complete unit to Bosnia in 1997 and Kosovo in 1999.

From 2004, the division began a series of deployments to Iraq and Afghanistan as part of the 'Global War on Terrorism'. Its aviation component was re-organised into a standard combat aviation brigade in 2005. By then the division and all its component brigades had relocated from Germany back to Fort Riley.

The division is currently part of the III Armored Corps, which is the US Army's heavy armoured reserve force. As part of Operation Atlantic Resolve, the 1st Combat Aviation Brigade has deployed twice to Eastern Europe since 2019 to support NATO.

	Location	Helicopters/Aircraft/UAV	Unit Role
1st Combat Aviation Brigade (1st Infantry Division)			
Headquarters and Headquarters Company "Archangels"	Fort Riley, Kansas		
1st Squadron, 6th Cavalry Regiment "The Fighting Sixth"	Fort Riley, Kansas	AH-64E	Air Cavalry Reconaissance Squadron
1st Battalion, 1st Aviation Regiment "Gunfighters"	Fort Riley, Kansas	AH-64D	Attack/Reconnaissance Battalion
3rd Battalion, 1st Aviation Regiment "Nightmares"	Fort Riley, Kansas	UH-60	Assault Battalion
2nd Battalion, 1st Aviation Regiment "Fighting Eagles"	Fort Riley, Kansas	UH-60L, HH-60M, CH-47F	General Support Aviation Battalion
F Company, 1st Battalion, 1st Aviation Regiment "Fenix"	Fort Riley, Kansas	MC-1Q	UAS Company
601st Aviation Support Battalion "Hellions"	Fort Riley, Kansas		Ground Support Unit

2ND COMBAT AVIATION BRIGADE

The 2nd Combat Aviation Brigade is one of the core units of the Republic of Korea (ROK)-US Combined Forces Command (CFC), helping to deter attacks across the de-militarised zone by communist North Korean forces.

In 2015, the last armoured brigade combat team of the 2nd Infantry Division was de-activated, and its place taken by brigades on rotation from the continental United States. This left the division's aviation, artillery and support brigades as the only US Army formations permanently based in South Korea. A ROK brigade is also permanently assigned to the division.

The aviation brigade was formed in 2005 out of two aviation units, the 17th Aviation Brigade based in Korea and the Fort Hood-based 6th Cavalry Brigade (Air Combat).

Continuing tension on the Korean peninsula meant the brigade did not deploy from Korea to undertake tours of duty in Iraq or Afghanistan during the 'Global War on Terrorism'. It

LEFT: 2nd Infantry Division AH-64D Apache Longbow attack helicopters overfly Camp Humphreys' tower in South Korea, during a deterrent exercise in 2004. (US ARMY, STEVE DAVIS)

regularly takes part in exercises with ROK and other allied forces, including practising to intercept sea-borne North Korean special forces squads. It also routinely takes part in readiness alerts and anti-invasion drills.

Under the Korean Rotational Force concept, additional aviation units are also regularly deployed to South Korea to augment the 2nd Combat Aviation Brigade. The brigade is based at Camp Humphreys, just over 60 kilometres south of the ROK capital Seoul, with its helicopters flying from Desiderio Army Airfield.

BOTTOM: UH-60 Black Hawk helicopters of the 2nd Combat Aviation Brigade are trained and qualified to operate from Republic of Korea (ROK) Navy ships in support of ROK maritime special operations forces. (US ARMY, RICHARD KIM)

	Location	Helicopters/Aircraft/UAV	Unit Role
2nd Combat Aviation Brigade (2nd Infantry Division)			
Headquarters and Headquarters Company	Desiderio Army Airfield, South Korea		
5th Squadron, 17th Cavalry Regiment	Desiderio Army Airfield, South Korea	AH-64E	Air Cavalry Reconaissance Squadron
4th Battalion, 2nd Aviation Regiment Death Dealer"	Desiderio Army Airfield, South Korea	AH-64E	Attack/Reconnaissance Battalion
2rd Battalion, 2nd Aviation Regiment "Wild Card"	Desiderio Army Airfield, South Korea	UH-60	Assault Battalion
3rd Battalion, 2nd Aviation Regiment "Nightmare"	Desiderio Army Airfield, South Korea	UH-60L, HH-60M, CH-47F	General Support Aviation Battalion
F Company, 2nd Aviation Regiment (MQ-1C)	Desiderio Army Airfield, South Korea	MC-1Q	UAS Company
602d Aviation Support Battalion	Desiderio Army Airfield, South Korea		Ground Support Unit

3RD COMBAT AVIATION BRIGADE

The 3rd Infantry Division earned the nickname 'Rock of the Marne', thanks to its steadfast defence of the French river against a German offensive in July 1918. As a result, its aviation component is known as 'Marne Air'.

The division's first aviation company was formed in July 1957 as it was preparing to deploy to Germany to build up NATO's defences. Its aviation component was expanded in 1984 when its aviation brigade was provisionally activated as the US Army's first dedicated aviation brigade in a mechanised infantry division.

It missed the 1991 Gulf War and in 1996 was relocated back to the continental United States as part of a major re-organisation of the US Army, with the aviation brigade taking up residence at Hunter Army Airfield in Georgia.

In 2003, the 3rd Infantry Division and its aviation brigade led the US Army's advance to Baghdad

during Operation Iraqi Freedom. During this period of intense combat, the division's McDonnell Douglas AH-64D Apaches were heavily involved in attacks on Iraqi tank divisions deployed to defend their capital.

In 2004, the unit was redesigned as the US Army's first modular combat aviation brigade, configured to a standard organisation to allow rotation through overseas deployments as part of the 'Global War on Terrorism'.

	Location	Helicopters/Aircraft/UAV	Unit Role
3rd Combat Aviation Brigade (3rd Infantry Division)			
Headquarters and Headquarters Company	Fort Stewart, Georgia		
3rd Squadron, 17th Cavalry Regiment "Lighthorse"	Fort Stewart, Georgia	AH-64E	Air Cavalry Reconaissance Squadron
4th Battalion, 3rd Aviation Regiment "Brawlers"	Fort Stewart, Georgia	UH-60	Attack/Reconnaissance Battalion
2nd Battalion, 3rd Aviation Regiment "Knighthawks"	Fort Stewart, Georgia	UH-60L HH-60M CH-47F	Assault Battalion
E Company, 3rd Aviation Regiment "Chaos"	Fort Stewart, Georgia	MC-1Q	General Support Aviation Battalion
603rd Aviation Support Battalion "Workhorse"	Fort Stewart, Georgia		UAS Company Ground Support Unit

	Location	Helicopters/Aircraft/UAV	Unit Role
4th Combat Aviation Brigade (4th Infantry Division)			
Headquarters and Headquarters Company	Fort Carson, Colorado		
6th Squadron, 17th Cavalry Regiment "Out Front"	Fort Carson, Colorado	AH-64E	Air Cavalry Reconaissance Squadron
4th Battalion, 4th Aviation Regiment "Gamblers"	Fort Carson, Colorado	AH-64D	Attack/Reconnaissance Battalion
3rd Battalion, 4th Aviation Regiment "Comanches"	Fort Carson, Colorado	UH-60	Assault Battalion
2nd Battalion, 4th Aviation Regiment "Mustangs"	Fort Carson, Colorado	UH-60L, HH-60M, CH-47F	General Support Aviation Battalion
F Company, 4th Aviation Regiment	Fort Carson, Colorado	MC-1Q	UAS Company
404th Aviation Support Battalion	Fort Carson, Colorado		Ground Support Unit

LEFT: 4th Infantry Division UH-60 Blackhawks stage an air assault during training near the Mihail Kogalniceanu Air Base in Romania as part of NATO exercises in 2018. (US ARMY, SPC ANDREW MCNEIL)

4TH COMBAT AVIATION BRIGADE

The 4th Infantry Division is currently based at Fort Carson, Colorado, as part of the III Armored Corps, which is America's heavy armoured reserve. It is nicknamed the 'Ivy' division in a play on words of the Roman numeral IV or 4.

The 'Ivy Eagles', as the division's aviators are known, trace their history back to the 4th Aviation Company, 4th Infantry Division, which was activated at Fort Lewis in Washington State in April 1957. It was expanded to the 4th Aviation Battalion in 1963 as part of the build-up to the Vietnam war. By the 1980s, the division's fourth brigade was assigned as its dedicated aviation component. During the 1990s it was designated as the US Army's experimental division before reverting to being a mechanised infantry division in 2001.

During the 'Global War on Terrorism', the division and its combat aviation brigade deployed on several occasions to Iraq and Afghanistan. In 2011, as part of US Army restructuring, the 4th Infantry Division re-located from Fort Hood in Texas to Fort Carson, Colorado. As part of this exercise, the 4th Combat Aviation Brigade was temporarily de-activated for two years until being stood up again in July 2013.

The brigade deployed in June 2018 to Europe to support the Operation Atlantic Resolve mission to conduct multinational training with NATO allies in Bulgaria, Estonia, Hungary, Latvia, Lithuania, Poland and Romania.

BELOW: A CH-47 Chinook of the 4th Combat Aviation Brigade took part in a special operations forces exercise at Nellis Air Force Base in Nevada in 2017. (US ARMY, STAFF SGT DANIEL CARTER)

	Location	Helicopters/Aircraft/UAV	Unit Role
10th Combat Aviation Brigade (10th Mountain Division)			
Headquarters and Headquarters Company	Fort Drum, New York		
6th Squadron, 6th Cavalry Regiment "Six Shooters"	Fort Drum, New York	AH-64E	Air Cavalry Reconaissance Squadron
1st Battalion, 10th Aviation Regiment "Dragons"	Fort Drum, New York	AH-64D	Attack/Reconnaissance Battalion
2nd Battalion, 10th Aviation Regiment "Knighthawks"	Fort Drum, New York	UH-60	Assault Battalion
3rd Battalions, 10th Aviation Regiment "Phoenix"	Fort Drum, New York	UH-60L, HH-60M, CH-47F	General Support Aviation Battalion
D Company, 10th Aviation Regiment	Fort Drum, New York	MC-1Q	UAS Company
277th Aviation Support Battalion "Mountain Eagle"	Fort Drum, New York		Ground Support Unit

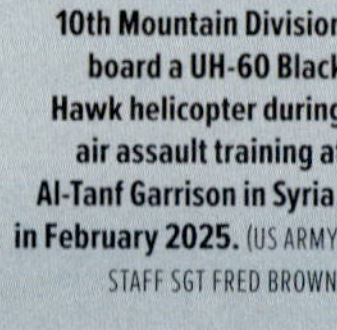

10TH COMBAT AVIATION BRIGADE

The 10th Mountain Division is part of the XVIII Airborne Corps, which is trained and equipped to deploy rapidly to global crisis zones. The division was originally formed in 1943 to fight in the mountains of Italy. It was disbanded after the end of the war, but reformed as an infantry formation between 1948 and 1955.

The division was reformed as a light infantry unit in 1985 and adopted the 10th Mountain title. Its aviation brigade was formed in 1988 and supported its parent division on operational deployments in the 1990s to Somalia, Haiti, Bosnia and Kosovo.

In 2002, the division was one of the first US Army formations to deploy to Afghanistan to establish the enduring American presence in the country, but it was not until 2003 that the full aviation brigade arrived at Bagram Air Base, near the central Asian country's capital Kabul.

Over the next decade the brigade and its units repeatedly deployed to Iraq and Afghanistan to fight in the 'Global War on Terrorism'.

In 2017, the full brigade deployed to Poland as part of the expanded Operation Atlantic Resolve to support NATO allies.

Since returning from that six-month deployment, the brigade has trained to rapidly deploy to crisis zones around the world from its Fort Drum base in upstate New York.

11TH AIRBORNE DIVISION

The 11th Airborne Division's Arctic Aviation Command (AAC) controls all aviation elements in Alaska and is trained and equipped to operate in extreme cold weather, mountainous and high latitude environments.

As a result of the 2022 redesignation of the United States Army Alaska Headquarters as the 11th Airborne Division (Arctic), moves were made to re-group aviation units into a single organisation. The AAC was activated in August 2024, and it is essentially equivalent in structure to a combat aviation brigade.

The AAC is a continuation of the rich history of US Army rotary-wing aviation in Alaska that dates back to 1958 with the arrival of the first Boeing-Vertol CH-21 Shawnee in Alaska.

In 2005, Task Force 49 (TF 49), a brigade-level aviation task force named after the 49th State, was established at Fort Wainwright. Four years later, Task Force 49 was deactivated and used as a base organisation for the newly formed 16th Combat Aviation Brigade, which was initially stationed in Alaska before moving to Washington State in 2011.

McDonnell Douglas AH-64D Apache attack helicopters and General Atomics MQ-1C Gray Eagle unmanned aerial vehicles arrived in Alaska in 2015, as part of the expansion of aviation capabilities in the Arctic.

ABOVE: Arctic Aviation Command CH-47Fs of the 52nd Aviation Regiment are fitted with winter skids so they can land in snow. (US ARMY, FORT WAINWRIGHT PAO)

LEFT: AH-64 Apache have been based in Alaska for a decade as part of a drive to beef up defences in the Arctic under the command of the 11th Airborne Division. (US ARMY, PFC BRANDON VASQUEZ)

	Location	Helicopters/Aircraft/UAV	Unit Role
Arctic Aviation Command (11th Airbrone Division)			
Headquarters and Headquarters Company	Fort Wainwright, Alaska		
1st Battalion, 25th Aviation Regiment	Fort Wainwright, Alaska	AH-64E	Attack/Reconnaissance Battalin
1st Battalion, 52nd Aviation Regiment	Fort Wainwright, Alaska	UH-60L, HH-60M, CH-47F	General Support Aviation Battalion
D Company, 25th Aviation Regiment "Gray Eagle"	Fort Wainwright, Alaska	MC-1Q	UAS Company
343d Aviation Support Detachment (Maintenance)	Fort Wainwright, Alaska		Ground Support Unit

	Location	Helicopters/Aircraft/UAV	Unit Role
25th Combat Aviation Brigade (25th Infantry Division)			
Headquarters and Headquarters Company (HHC)	Wheeler Army Airfield, Hawaii		
2nd Squadron, 6th Cavalry Regiment "Lightning Horse"	Wheeler Army Airfield, Hawaii	AH-64E, RQ-7	Air Cavalry Reconaissance Squadron
2nd Battalion, 25th Aviation Regiment "Diamondhead"	Wheeler Army Airfield, Hawaii	UH-60	Attack/Reconnaissance Battalion
3rd Battalion, 25th Aviation Regiment "Hammerhead"	Wheeler Army Airfield, Hawaii	UH-60L, HH-60M, CH-47F	Assault Battalion
D Company, 25th Aviation Regiment	Wheeler Army Airfield, Hawaii	MC-1Q	General Support Aviation Battalion
209th Aviation Support Battalion "Lobos"	Wheeler Army Airfield, Hawaii		UAS Company Ground Support Unit

25TH COMBAT AVIATION BRIGADE

The 25th Infantry Division, nicknamed 'Tropic Lightning', has had a long association with the US Pacific Island State of Hawaii after being originally stood up at Schofield Barracks outside Honolulu on Oahu in 1941.

It fought across the Pacific in World War Two and then served in the Korean War. Helicopters carried Tropic Lightning troops into battle in Vietnam beginning its long association with air mobility.

In 1985, the division's aviation battalion was expanded to a full aviation brigade equipped with Sikorsky UH-60 Black Hawks and McDonnell Douglas AH-64A Apache attack helicopters. The brigade is based at Wheeler Army Airfield. Currently, it only has one attack helicopter battalion, rather than the standard two AH-64 battalions, as one was re-located to Alaska in 2015.

During the 'Global War on Terrorism', the brigade and its units regularly deployed to Afghanistan, Iraq and Syria to support US military operations in these countries.

The focus of the brigade is now on operating across the Pacific region and its helicopter crews are trained and qualified to conduct long-range over-water air assault missions, as well as flying off US Navy warships. The brigade's units also routinely deploy to South Korea to reinforce allied troops in the country.

Its attack helicopter crews are in the process of converting to the new Echo variant of the AH-64.

RIGHT: A 25th Combat Aviation Brigade CH-47 Chinook helicopter lands on the deck of the ex-USS *Tarawa* during a non-combatant evacuation exercise. (US ARMY, CAPT HEBA BULLOCK)

BELOW: AH-64 Apache helicopters fly in formation around Oahu in May 2019 to commemorate the 158th anniversary of the 2nd Squadron, 6th Cavalry Regiment's activation. (US ARMY, SGT RYAN JENKINS)

82ND COMBAT AVIATION BRIGADE

The 82nd Airborne Division 'All American' is the US Army's global response unit, which is held at readiness to deploy anywhere in the world at very short notice. Its ready brigade, which includes a battalion-sized aviation task force, is able to be airborne out of its Fort Bragg base in North Carolina in 18 hours.

The ready aviation task force is trained and equipped to rapidly load its helicopters on to US Air Force transport aircraft from nearby Pope Field for deployment to overseas crisis zones. After the first echelon of 82nd Airborne's paratroopers seize an airfield, transport aircraft carrying the aviation task force's helicopters can land and within a few hours its aviators will be in action.

The division's 'All American' title comes from its heritage in World War One, when it was formed with personnel and units from every one of America's states. It 1942, it became the first US Army airborne division under the command of the famous Major General Matthew Ridgway, jumping into battle in Sicily, Normandy and Holland.

After World War Two, it remained in the airborne role and became the US Army's strategic reserve division. In this role it has seen action in numerous exercises and conflicts over the past 80 years. The division received its first helicopters in 1957, and its aviation component was expanded to brigade strength in 1987. The current combat aviation brigade has adopted the title 'Pegasus' in honour of the role of allied airborne forces in the 1944 Normandy invasion. During the 'Global War on Terrorism', the brigade and its units have seen regular service in Iraq, Afghanistan and Syria. ➤

AH-64A attack helicopters prepare to take-off during Operation Desert Shield in the build-up to the 1991 Gulf War. (US ARMY)

A CH-47F of the 82nd Combat Aviation Brigade's 82nd Combat Aviation Brigade during an air assault exercise. (US ARMY)

	Location	Helicopters/Aircraft/UAV	Unit Role
82nd Combat Aviation Brigade (82nd Airborne Division "All American")			
Headquarters and Headquarters Company "Gryphon"	Fort Bragg, North Carolina		
1st Squadron, 17th Cavalry Regiment "Saber"	Fort Bragg, North Carolina	AH-64E, RQ-7	Air Cavalry Reconnaissance Squadron
1st Battalion, 82nd Aviation Regiment "Wolfpack"	Fort Bragg, North Carolina	AH-64E	Attack/Reconnaissance Battalin
2nd Battalion, 82nd Aviation Regiment "Corsair" (UH-60M)	Fort Bragg, North Carolina	UH-60	Assault Battalion
3rd Battalion, 82nd Aviation Regiment "Talon" (UH-60L HH-60M CH-47)	Fort Bragg, North Carolina	UH-60L, HH-60M, CH-47F	General Support Aviation Battalion
D Company, 82nd Aviation Regiment (MQ-1C)	Fort Bragg, North Carolina	MC-1Q	UAS Company
122nd Aviation Support Battalion "Atlas"			Ground Support Unit

101ST COMBAT AVIATION BRIGADE

The 101st Airborne Division (Air Assault) is the US Army's only dedicated air assault formation. Its traces its roots back to World War One and was the second US Army airborne division to be formed in 1942. It saw action in Normandy and Holland in 1944 and was the inspiration for the *Band of Brothers* television series. Its iconic 'Screaming Eagles' nickname comes from the division's bald eagle badge that dates from the Civil War.

During the Vietnan war it converted to the air mobile role; when it returned home to Fort Campbell in Kentucky it was permanently assigned the air assault role as part of XVIII Airborne Corps. It was equipped with enough helicopters to move an entire brigade in one lift.

The division carried out complex air assault operations in the 1991 and 2003 Iraq wars. In 2005, as a result of the 'Global War on Terrorism', the division's helicopter assets were reduced and redistributed around other units to allow a more balanced rotation of aviation units to Iraq and Afghanistan.

The 101st Combat Aviation Brigade then took its place in regular rotations of aviation units to Iraq and Afghanistan. In 2020, the brigade deployed to Poland under the banner of Operation Atlantic Resolve to support NATO.

In 2024, plans were announced to provide the brigade with additional Boeing CH-47F Chinooks to restore its ability to move a full brigade in one lift.

RIGHT: Fort Campbell in Kentucky has been the home of the 'Screaming Eagles' of the 101st Airborne Division since 1956. (US ARMY, SAM SHORE)

BOTTOM: 101st Airborne Division AH-64E Apache helicopters being refuelled during a large-scale, long-range air assault at the Joint Readiness Training Center at Fort Polk in Louisiana. (US ARMY, CAPT HAYLEY HAKA)

	Location	Helicopters/Aircraft/UAV	Unit Role
101st Combat Aviation Brigade (101st Airborne Division (Air Assault) "Screaming Eagles")			
Headquarters and Headquarters Company "Hell Cats"	Fort Campbell, Kentucky		
2nd Squadron, 17th Cavalry Regiment "Out Front"	Fort Campbell, Kentucky	AH-64E, RQ-7	Air Cavalry Reconaissance Squadron
1st Battalion, 101st Aviation Regiment"Expect No Mercy"	Fort Campbell, Kentucky	AH-64E	Attack/Reconnaissance Battalion
5th Battalion, 101st Aviation Regiment "Eagle Assault"	Fort Campbell, Kentucky	UH-60	Assault Battalion
6th Battalion, 101st Aviation Regiment "Shadow of the Eagle"	Fort Campbell, Kentucky	UH-60L, HH-60M, CH-47F	General Support Aviation Battalion
B Company, 101 Aviation Regiment "Archangels"	Fort Campbell, Kentucky	MC-1Q	UAS Company
96th Aviation Support Battalion "Troubleshooters"	Fort Campbell, Kentucky		Ground Support Unit

	Location	Helicopters/Aircraft/UAV	Unit Role
12th Combat Aviation Brigade (V Corps)			
Headquarters and Headquarters Company	Katterbach Army Airfield, Ansbach, Germany		
1st Battalion, 3rd Aviation Regiment "Viper"	Katterbach Army Airfield, Ansbach, Germany	AH-64E	Attack/Reconnaissance Battalion
1st Battalion, 214th Aviation Regiment Battalion "Cougar"	Wiesbaden Army Airfield, Germany	UH-60L HH-60M CH-47	General Support Aviation Battalion
C Company "Dust Off"	Grafenwöhr Army Airfield, Germany	HH-60M	
B Company "Big Windy"	Katterbach Army Airfield, Ansbach, Germany	CH-47F	
D Company "Skymasters"	Wiesbaden & Katterbach Army Airfield, Germany		Aviation Support
E Company "Barons"	Wiesbaden Army Airfield, Germany	C-12U Huron, UC-35A	Theatre Aviation Support

12TH COMBAT AVIATION BRIGADE

The brigade traces its history back to the 12th Aviation Group, which was formed in 1965 at the height of the Vietnam war. After service in Southeast Asia and then a period assigned to support the XVIII Airborne Corps at Fort Bragg in North Carolina, it moved to Europe in 1979.

Since then, the brigade has been permanently based in Europe as the main aviation element of the US Army's V Corps. In 1988, it entered a new era when the 5th Squadron, 6th Cavalry Regiment arrived in Europe with McDonnell Douglas AH-64A Apache attack helicopters. This heralded the start of its role as an attack helicopter formation, configured and equipped to carry out deep attacks behind enemy lines.

The brigade took its Apache to the Middle East in time for Operation Desert Storm and worked alongside the 101st Airborne Division

(Air Assault) during its mission to outflank the Iraqi army in Kuwait.

In 1999, it dispatched a task force to Albania during the Kosovo War. During the 'Global War on Terrorism', the brigade and its units made regular deployments to Iraq, Afghanistan and Syria. After the 2014 Russian occupation of Crimea, it played an important role in supporting NATO's deterrent exercises across Eastern Europe.

LEFT: The 1st Attack Reconnaissance Battalion is the core striking power of the 12th Combat Aviation Brigade. (US ARMY, ERICH BACKES)

BELOW: The 12th Combat Aviation Brigade is the US Army's only permanently assigned aviation formation based in Europe. (US ARMY, VISUAL INFORMATION SPECIALIST ERICH BACKES)

	Location	Helicopters/Aircraft/UAV	Unit Role
16th Combat Aviation Brigade			
Headquarters and Headquarters Company	Joint Base Lewis McChord, WA		
4th Squadron, 6th Cavalry Regiment	Joint Base Lewis McChord, WA	AH-64E	Air Cavalry Reconaissance Squadron
1st Battalion, 229th Aviation Regiment	Joint Base Lewis McChord, WA	AH-64E	Attack/Reconnaissance Battalion
2nd Battalion, 158th Aviation Regiment	Joint Base Lewis McChord, WA	UH-60	Assault Battalion
1st Battalion, 52nd Aviation Regiment	Joint Base Lewis McChord, WA	UH-60L, HH-60M, CH-47F	General Support Aviation Battalion
D Company, 25th Aviation Regiment	Joint Base Lewis McChord, WA	MC-1Q	UAS Company
46th Aviation Support Battalion	Joint Base Lewis McChord, WA		Ground Support Unit

16TH COMBAT AVIATION BRIGADE

The 16th Combat Aviation Brigade is home-garrisoned at Joint Base Lewis–McChord (JBLM) in Washington State on the Pacific coast. It is under the command of the 7th Infantry Division, which is responsible for the training and sustainment of units assigned to reinforce US Indo-Pacific Command in time of crisis or conflict.

US war plans call for units based on the west coast of the continental United States to be rapidly mobilised and then deployed to South Korea or elsewhere in the Pacific region.

It was first formed in 1968 and then deployed to the Da Nang region of South Vietnam for the final years of the conflict in Southeast Asia. After it returned home, the brigade was disbanded.

The expansion of the US Army units in Alaska led to the formation of an aviation task force at Fort Wainwright in 2005. Four years later, the aviation task force in Alaska was expanded and it was placed under the command of the newly reformed 16th Combat Aviation Brigade at JBLM. By 2014, the 16th Brigade was fully up to strength, and it cut its ties with the Alaska-based aviation task force.

The brigade routinely trains with allies from across the Pacific region in joint exercises to perfect its ability to operate in littoral terrain. Aircrew from the brigade are all trained to operate over water and have deck-landing qualifications to land their helicopters on US Navy ships.

TRAINING AND SUPPORT UNITS

Outside the main combat aviation brigades, the US Army operates dozens of helicopters, aircraft and unmanned aerial vehicles in training, support and trials roles.

The US Army's National Training Center at Fort Irwin in California and the Joint Readiness Training Center at Fort Polk, Louisiana, both have detachments of helicopters to provide medical evacuation, safety and administrative support.

US Army Operational Test Command and US Army Test and Evaluation Command (ATEC) operate fleets of helicopters and aircraft to assist in bringing new air vehicles, weapons and on-board sensors into service or test modifications to existing platforms. These organisations employ many of the US Army's best aviators and engineers to ensure new equipment lives up to expectations, is safe to fly and can be used to best effect.

One of the most high-profile US Army aviation units is the 12th Aviation Battalion, based at Davison Army Airfield, Fort Belvoir, Virginia. This unit has a fleet of Sikorsky UH-60 Black Hawk helicopters, including several VH-60M VIP transport variants, to move senior US Army leaders around the Washington DC area. The unit received prominence when one of the battalion's UH-60Ls was involved in a mid-air collision with American Airlines aircraft over the River Potomac, close to Reagan National Airport, in January 2025.

ABOVE: A 12th Aviation Battalion UH-60L was lost in a tragic collision with an airliner over the Potomac River on January 29, 2025. (US COAST GUARD)

BOTTOM: VH-60M Black Hawks of the 12th Aviation Battalion flies VIPs around the Washington DC area. (ACROTERION)

	Location	Helicopters/Aircraft/UAV	Unit Role
Joint Readiness Training Center			
5th Aviation Battalion	Fort Polk, Lousiana	UH-72, UH-60A	Training Support
National Training Center			
2916th Aviation Battalion, 916th Support Brigade	Fort Irwin, California	UH-60	Training Support
B Company, 229th Aviation Regiment	Fort Irwin, California	MQ-1C	Training Support

The 'Night Stalkers'

160th Special Operations Aviation Regiment (Airborne)

ABOVE: The MH-47E is the work horse of the 160th SOAR(A). This Chinook is landing on the USS *Kearsarge* during a training exercise. (US NAVY)

The 160th Special Operations Aviation Regiment (Airborne), or SOAR(A) and known as the 'Night Stalkers', is organised into four battalions, which each comprise a number of companies operating different types of aircraft, helicopters and unmanned aerial vehicles. It has some 3,000 personnel and operates nearly 200 helicopters. The battalions and companies are organised in such a way as to allow them to operate independently for prolonged periods, including rapidly deployable command and repair elements.

A full spectrum of combat aviation capabilities is represented within the 160th SOAR(A), including Boeing MH-6M Little Bird, Sikorsky MH-60M Black Hawk DAP for attack, and MH-60M and Boeing MH-47G Chinooks for aerial assault and transport. Surveillance and strike capabilities are provided by the General Atomics MQ-1C Gray Eagle unmanned aerial vehicle.

All the 160th SOAR(A) battalions are based in the continental USA so must deploy by air to overseas operations by USAF C-5 Galaxy or C-17 Globemaster aircraft. The MH-6Ms are also routinely deployed to remote locations and are lifted by C-130J Hercules transport aircraft. No-notice rapid deployment exercises are a key part of the regiment's training cycle.

Fort Campbell in Kentucky is home to the regiment's headquarters, as well as conversion and training units and the MQ-1C drone companies.

The 160th Regiment is the main deployable combat unit of the United States Army Special Operations Aviation Command (USASOAC), which also has several other aviation elements.

Utility and communications support is provided by the US Army

RIGHT: The 160th SOAR(A) now rarely deploys without support from the MQ-1C of Echo Company. (US ARMY)

Special Operations Command Flight Company (UFC), which operates a mix of non-combat aircraft and helicopters. These include UH-60L Black Hawks, C-212 Aviocars, C-27J Spartans, UV-20 Porters and C-12C Hurons. A key task is providing jump aircraft for US Army Special Forces students at the John F Kennedy Special Warfare Center and School at Fort Bragg in North Carolina. On average, its aircraft enable 30,000 parachute jumps a year to take place.

Before US Army aviators and maintainers can take their place in the 160th SOAR(A) they have to undergo an intense training programme run by USASOAC's own Special Operations Training Battalion (SOATB). Students are usually experienced aviators even before they apply to join the 160th SOAR(A).

SOATB conducts basic Army Special Operations Aviation (ARSOA) individual training and provides education in order to produce crew members and support personnel with basic and advanced qualifications for the 160th SOAR(A). Some 80 officers and 325 enlisted personnel are trained each year by the SOATB.

ARSOA's Technology Applications Program Office (TAPO) at Joint Base Langley-Eustis in Virginia is responsible for managing its helicopters, aircraft and other equipment from its initial procurement through to in-service logistic support and upgrade before preparing it for disposal.

	Location	Helicopters/Aircraft/UAV
US Army Special Operations Aviation Command		
160th Special Operations Aviation Regiment (Airborne) "Night Stalkers"		
Headquarters and Headquarters Company	Fort Campbell, Kentucky	
1st Battalion	Fort Campbell, Kentucky	MH-60M, MH-60M DAP, MH-6M, AH-6M
2nd Battalion	Fort Campbell, Kentucky	MH-60M, HM-47G
3rd Battalion	Hunter Army Airfield, Georgia	MH-60M, HM-47G
4th Battalion	Gray AAF/Joint Base Lewis-McChord, Washington	MH-60M, HM-47G
F Company, 160th SOAR (A)	Fort Campbell, Kentucky	MC-1Q
E Company, 160th SOAR (A)	Fort Campbell, Kentucky	MC-1Q
USASOC Flight Company	Fort Bragg, North Carolina	C-127J, CASA 212, UH-60L, C-12C, C-12J

LEFT: AH/MH-6 Little Bird provides agile battlefield mobility to small contingents of US Special Operations Forces. (US ARMY)

At Fort Campbell, the ARSOA Systems Integration Management Office (SIMO) is responsible for developing requirements for new equipment and the long-term planning of future procurement.

BELOW: An MH-60M Black Hawk lands a US Army Special Forces detachment on a US Navy submarine. (US NAVY)

ABOVE: US Army Military Intelligence operates a fleet of manned surveillance aircraft, including de Havilland Dash 8 aircraft. (MARK HARKIN)

RIGHT: (SAKAI JIN)

Watching the Enemy

Military intelligence units

Building up intelligence on enemy forces, insurgent militias and non-state groups such as drugs cartels, is the job of the US Army Military Intelligence.

It has long operated a fleet of surveillance aircraft to carry out the worldwide aerial exploitation (AE) and aerial reconnaissance (AR) missions for the US Army and other agencies of the US government, including the National Security Agency (NSA) and the Central Intelligence Agency (CIA). The US Army aviation branch provides pilots and aircraft maintenance personnel, while Military Intelligence supplies intelligence analysts and other specialist personnel.

Today, US Army Intelligence and Security Command (INSCOM) is responsible for aircraft used in AE and AR roles. Its fleet is assigned to two Military Intelligence brigades, one based in the continental United States and the other in South Korea.

The main AE and AR formation is the 116th Military Intelligence Brigade (Aerial Intelligence), which is headquartered at Fort Gordon in Georgia. The unit has a long tradition dating back to 1946 went it was first formed, but it was only activated for its current role in August 2014.

Its flying operations are spread across four locations to allow its aircraft and unmanned aerial vehicles (UAVs) to train with US Army units in their home garrisons.

Cessna MC-12S Enhanced Medium Altitude Reconnaissance and

RIGHT: The 3rd Military Intelligence Battalion is forward based at Desiderio Army Airfield, Camp Humphreys in South Korea to monitor the demilitarised zone bordering the communist North. (US ARMY, KURT VAN SLOOTEN)

	Location	Helicopters/Aircraft/UAV	Unit Role
Intelligence and Security Command (INSCOM)			
116th Military Intelligence Brigade	Fort Gordon, Georgia		
A Company, 15th Military Intelligence Battalion	Fort Hood, Texas	MC-12S/RC-12X	Aerial Exploitation unit
B Company, 15th Military Intelligence Battalion	Fort Hood, Texas	MQ-1C	Aerial Exploitation unit
A Company, 204th Military Intelligence Battalion	Fort Bliss, Texas	EO-5	Aerial Exploitation unit
C Company, 204th Military Intelligence Battalion	Fort Bliss, Texas	MQ-1C	Aerial Exploitation unit
A Company, 224th Military Intelligence Battalion	Hunter Army Airfield, Georgia	MC-12S/RC-12X	Aerial Exploitation unit
B Company, 224th Military Intelligence Battalion	Hunter Army Airfield, Georgia	MQ-1C	Aerial Exploitation unit
501st Military Intelligence Brigade	Pyongtaek, Desiderio AAF, South Korea		
3rd Military Intelligence Battalion	Pyongtaek, Desiderio AAF, South Korea	EO-5C, EO-6A, RC-12X	Aerial Exploitation unit

Surveillance System (EMARSS-S) and General Atomics MQ-1C Gray Eagle UAVs are operated by the 15th Military Intelligence Battalion (AE) out of Fort Hood in Texas. The 204th Military Intelligence Battalion (AR) at Fort Bliss in Texas flies de Havilland Dash-7 and Dash-8 aircraft for surveillance and also operates MQ-1Cs. MC-12S and RC-12X platforms are flown by the 206th Military Intelligence Battalion (AE) at Fort Gordon.

The 224th Military Intelligence Battalion (AE) at Hunter Army Airfield in Georgia flies MC-12Ss, RC-12Xs and MQ-1Cs. The battalion has remained deployed in combat operations for several years and forward detachments have been reported operating in Chad, Guatemala and Colombia. Its MQ-1C company has carried out what are dubbed 'Remote Split Operations', with air vehicles being flown via satellite from command centres in the continental USA, being the first US Army unit to conduct these types of operations.

The 501st Military Intelligence Brigade conducts theatre intelligence gathering in support of Combined Forces Command (CFC) in South Korea with a mix of RC-12X and Dash-7/8 platforms.

A major programme is under way to replace the legacy fixed-wing surveillance aircraft fleet, but a unique procurement process is being followed. Three trials aircraft have been operating for at least two years in Europe and the Pacific theatre, under the auspices of two private contracts, which have provided aircraft and flight crews. Mission specialists are a mix of US Military Intelligence personnel and industry contractors.

ABOVE: US Army RC-12 Guardrail intelligence gathering aircraft operate around the world to build up an electronic order of battle of enemy radar systems and communications networks. (US AIR FORCE, AIRMAN FIRST CLASS ANDREW OQUENDO)

LEFT: The Airborne Reconnaissance and Targeting Exploitation Multi-Mission Intelligence System (ARTEMIS) aerial technology demonstrator is based on a modified Bombardier Challenger 650 aircraft. ARTEMIS is managed by its developer, the defence and technology company Leidos. (LEIDOS)

ABOVE: More than 200 UH-72 Lakotas are now used across the National Guard in non-combat support, medical evacuation and utility roles. (US ARMY)

Militia Aviators

Army National Guard

The National Guard traces its history back to colonial times in 1636 when the Massachusetts Bay Colony's General Court ordered the setting up of three militia regiments to defend what was then a British colony. Today, more than 325,000 Guardsmen serve in the Army National Guard (ARNG) and 107,000 serve the Air National Guard.

Those early militia units fought and won the War of Independence against the British and then formed the core of the Union and Confederate armies during the Civil War. At the start of the 20th century, moves were made to re-organise and standardise state militias so they could better support the regular army in times of conflict. A dedicated branch of the Department of the Army was set up to oversee federal support for the state National Guards. Today, this is known as the National Guard Bureau and its head is a four-star general and a member of the Joint Chiefs of Staff.

In World War One and Two, the bulk of the National Guard was mobilised to fight overseas. During the Cold War, the National Guard was further streamlined and trained to allow it to be rapidly mobilised to fight alongside its active-duty colleagues.

An important part of the National Guard mission is to support state authorities in time of local emergencies, natural disasters and civil unrest, under the Defense Support to Civilian Authorities (DSCA) mission. State National Guard units have a dual chain of command to their respective governors for local missions and to the federal government in time national emergency or war. Each state has its own military commander, known as the adjutant general, who reports to his governor. The exception to this is in the District of Columbia, which is not a state, so the United States president is the direct commander of

RIGHT: Hundreds of UH-60 Black Hawk helicopters are used by the National Guard in air assault and transport roles. (US AIR FORCE, CAPT DARIN OVERSTREET)

its National Guard, via the defence department.

The National Guard Bureau has its own budget, which pays for most of the equipment, fuel, ammunition and other materiel used by the reserve organisation. In 2025, federal spending on the ARNG ran to just under $10bn on pay, $8bn on operational activity and $2.2bn on buying new equipment. This is more than the total defence budgets of many NATO countries.

Since World War Two, the ARNG has become increasingly integrated with the activity-duty US Army, with specific ARNG units assigned to support overseas theatres of operation or active-duty units. For long periods, the ARNG had to make do with second-hand equipment that was considered obsolete by the active-duty force. In the 1980s, as the ARNG role was uprated it was given higher priority for new equipment, so its units can take their place as part of active-duty formations. During the 'Global War on Terrorism' over the past 25 years, this drive to bring reserve units up to active-duty standards accelerated as an increasing number of ARNG units were mobilised for service overseas.

Today the ARNG is organised around eight mechanised infantry divisions and each of these has its own combat aviation brigade, which generally flies the same types of helicopters as its active-duty counterparts.

Each ARNG combat aviation brigade contains at least one assault helicopter battalion flying Sikorsky UH-60 Black Hawks, and a general support aviation battalion flying a combination of Boeing CH-47F Chinooks and UH-60s. Four of the combat aviation brigades have an attack helicopter battalion, equipped with Boeing AH-64 Apache gunships. These are in the process of converting to the '64 Echo variant from the older Delta model.

There are also four separate ARNG aviation brigades that are configured to operate independently or outside of divisional control.

One major difference to active-duty combat aviation brigades is that until recently the ARNG had yet to field unmanned aerial vehicles. Funding was provided in 2023 to begin buying the General Atomics MQ-1C Gray Eagle, with 12 of the 25M variants being ordered as a first batch.

ARNG aviation units currently operate more than 72 AH-64s, 164 CH-47Fs and 900 UH-60 variants.

The ARNG Bureau supports the combat aviation brigades by funding operational flying and training, as well as purchasing new helicopters, weapons and spare parts.

In 2025, funding for ARNG aviation activity was $1.15bn – an increase over the previous year. However, procurement of new helicopters has slowed after reaching a high in 2023: more than $2bn was spent on 12 MQ-1Cs, 24 AH-64Es, 35 UH-60Ms and 24 UH-60L/V conversions that year. In 2024, 24 AH-64Es, 24 UH-60Ms and 26 UH-60L/Vs were ❯

ABOVE: The South Carolina Army National Guard operates C-26 Metroliners in the operational support mission, moving passengers and high-value cargo around the continental USA. (US ARMY NATIONAL GUARD, CAPT JESSICA DONNELLY)

BELOW: Reserve aviators from the National Guard's 29th Combat Aviation Brigade served in Iraq and Syria in 2017. (US ARMY)

funded but only 15 UH-60Ms were included in the 2025 National Guard Bureau budget.

The UH-60V programme allows ARNG aviation units to transition to the glass cockpit-equipped version of the iconic UH-60 Black Hawk, to replace its older UH-60A and L variants.

The first tactical unit to be fielded with the UH-60V was the Illinois Army National Guard's 1st Battalion of the 106th Aviation Regiment, which received the initial aircraft in July 2021 and began operating the helicopter the following year.

Although ARNG aviation units mirror the organisation of active-duty counterparts they are mostly based in small company or platoon-sized detachments deployed around the country, based in local communities to ensure they can recruit from as wide a pool of people as possible.

The ARNG also operates more than 212 Airbus UH-72A/B Lakota light utility helicopters, used primarily for non-combat roles in support of their state missions. This includes responding to floods and other natural disasters, helping law enforcement, medical evacuations and providing support to training exercises. The ARNG has bought 18 of

ABOVE: UH-72 Lakota and UH-60 Black Hawk helicopters have important missions to support civil authorities across the continental USA. (US AIR FORCE, TIM CHACON)

BELOW: UH-72 Lakota helicopters of the 36th Combat Aviation Brigade were mobilised to assist flooded communities north of Beaumont, Texas, on August 31, 2017, after Hurricane Harvey made landfall in southeastern Texas. (US ARMY NATIONAL GUARD, SGT 1ST CLASS MALCOLM MCCLENDON)

the upgraded UH-72B models and is considering buying more.

ARNG Lakota helicopters are grouped into six security and support battalions, which are distributed around the continental USA to ensure they can provide support to every state governor in times of crisis.

After US President Donald Trump was elected in January 2025, he ordered the US military to support his clampdown on border crossings by migrants into the United States. ARNG helicopters, primarily UH-72As and CH-47Fs, from the Texas National Guard were the first aviation units to be involved in expanding the border security mission.

ABOVE: South Carolina Forestry Commission and other response agencies asked the state's Army National Guard to provide helicopters to join the firefighting efforts in the Table Rock Complex, upstate South Carolina, in March 2025. (US ARMY NATIONAL GUARD, SGT 1ST CLASS ROBERTO DI GIOVINE)

LEFT: A UH-60 Black Hawk helicopter of the Pennsylvania Army National Guard's 28th Combat Aviation Brigade at Muir Army Airfield during a training exercise at Fort Indiantown Gap in July 2022. (US ARMY NATIONAL GUARD, SPC JOHN TRAPANI)

Supporting the States

ARNG Combat Aviation Brigades

RIGHT: Kentucky National Guard UH-60 crews prepare to launch their helicopters during a training exercise at Fort Bliss in Texas. (TEXAS ARMY NATIONAL GUARD, SGT TOM HARRINGTON)

BELOW: The UH-60 Black Hawk is the mainstay of Army National Guard air assault units. (US ARMY, SGT 1ST CLASS RYAN SHELDON)

The Army National Guard's (ARNG) 12 combat aviation brigades trace their roots back to the air observation units established during World War Two to spot artillery batteries. During the 1970s, the ARNG aviation units started to receive significant numbers of helicopters, including Bell UH-1 utility, Boeing CH-47 Chinook heavy-lift and Bell AH-1 Cobra gunships left over from the Vietnam War.

The downsizing of the active-duty US Army after the ending of the Cold War led to another big wave of equipment transfers to the ARNG, including the first Sikorsky UH-60 Black Hawk utility and McDonnell Douglas AH-64A Apache attack helicopters. After 2005, the ARNG divisions were re-organised to match active-duty division structures and standardised aviation units were established to improve inter-operability.

28th Combat Aviation Brigade (28th Infantry Division)		
Headquarters and Headquarters Company (Muir Army Airfield, Pennsylvania)		
2nd Battalion, 104th Aviation Regiment	UH-60, CH-47F	General Support Aviation Battalion
29th Combat Aviation Brigade (29th Infantry Division)		
Headquarters and Headquarters Company (Edgewood, Maryland)		
2nd Battalion, 224th Aviation Regiment	UH-60, CH-47F	Assault Battalion
1st Battalion, 111th Aviation Regiment	UH-60, CH-47F	General Support Aviation Battalion
248th Aviation Support Battalion		Ground Support Unit
34th Expeditionary Combat Aviation Brigade (34th Infantry Division)		
Headquarters and Headquarters Company (St Pauls, Minnisota)		
2nd Battalion, 147th Aviation Regiment	UH-60	Assault Battalion
2nd Battalion, 211th Aviation Regiment	UH-60, CH-47F	General Support Aviation Battalion
35th Combat Aviation Brigade (35th Infantry Division)		
Headquarters and Headquarters Company (Sedalia, Missouri)		
1st Battalion, 106th Aviation Regiment	UH-60	Assault Battalion
1st Battalion, 135th Aviation Regiment	UH-60	Assault Battalion
1st Battalion, 112th Aviation Regiment	UH-60, UH-72	Security & Support Battalion
935th Aviation Support Battalion		Ground Support Unit

In April 2025, US Defense Secretary Pete Hegseth announced a shake-up of the Army National Guard, including disbandment of two aviation brigades, although the specific units were not identified.

The 28th Combat Aviation Brigade is headquartered in Pennsylvania. It was first stood up as a brigade in 1986 and its units were mobilised to serve in Iraq and Syria in 2009 and 2022.

ARNG aviators from Arizona, Kentucky and Virginia serve in the 29th Combat Aviation Brigade, headquartered in Maryland.

The 34th Combat Aviation Brigade is headquartered in Minnesota and comprises aviation units from the US Midwest, including air assault and general support units. In 2024, plans were announced to covert the formation into a new Heavy Combat Aviation Brigade, which will add two AH-64 Apache helicopter attack battalions.

The Missouri-headquartered 35th Combat Aviation Brigade comprises two assault aviation battalions to support ARNG units in the US Midwest. It was mobilised in 2018 to command US Army aviation units taking part in Operation Inherent Resolve in Iraq, Syria and Jordan.

The 36th Combat Aviation Brigade is part of the Texas ARNG and comprises units from across the several southern states, including Texas, Arkansas and Alabama. It deployed to Iraq in 2007 for a year-long combat tour of duty and

ABOVE: Army National Guard aviators from the 36th Combat Aviation Brigade carried out joint exercises with the US Navy in the Arabian Gulf in 2023, carrying out deck landing qualifications on USS *Lewis B Puller*. (US NAVY, SN CHRISTOPHER PARANDHAMAIA)

LEFT: More than 200 UH-72s are used by Army National Guard units to support civil authorities around the continental United States. (SKUZBUCKET)

ABOVE: A UH-72 from the Nebraska National Guard conducts water rescue training during an exercise in 2017 at Fort McCoy in Wisconsin. (US AIR NATIONAL GUARD, MASTER SGT KELLEN KROENING)

ABOVE RIGHT: US Marines trained with the Indiana National Guard in March 2025 in casualty evacuation exercises. (US MARINE CORPS, MAJ LARA SOTO)

then to Kuwait in 2013 under Operation Spartan Shield.

The California National Guard's 40th Combat Aviation Brigade is headquartered in Stockton and controls aviation units from the US West Coast. It deployed to Iraq and Syria in 2021 for Operation Inherent Resolve.

From its headquarters in Latham, New York, the 42nd Combat Aviation Brigade controls ARNG aviation units in 11 states on the US East Coast. The brigade deployed to Iraq in 2004 and Afghanistan in 2013.

The ARNG has four separate aviation brigades, each having a distinct role and unique configuration.

In Little Rock, Arkansas, the 63rd Theatre Aviation Brigade holds the support mission within the continental USA and US Southern Command.

The 185th Aviation Brigade is headquartered in Jackson, Mississippi, and controls units from across the Southern states. It deployed to Iraq in 2023 for Operation Inherent Resolve.

The 77th Expeditionary Aviation Brigade, headquartered in Camp Robinson, Arkansas, comprises a security and support battalion, flying the Airbus UH-72A Lakota and several ground support units. It is configured to be expanded and to take under command more aviation units – this occurred when it

36th Combat Aviation Brigade (36th Infantry Division)		
Headquarters and Headquarters Company (Bergstrom AFRC, Texas)		
1st Battalion, 149th Aviation Regiment	AH-64E	Attack/Reconnaissance Battalion
1st Battalion, 108th Aviation Regiment	UH-60	Assault Battalion
2nd Battalion, 149th Aviation Regiment	UH-60,CH-47F	General Support Aviation Battalion
449th Aviation Support Battalion		Ground Support Unit
38th Combat Aviation Brigade (38th Infantry Division)		
Headquarters and Headquarters Company (Shelbyville, Indiana)		
1st Battalion, 137th Aviation Regiment	UH-60	Assault Battalion
2nd Battalion, 238th Aviation Regiment	UH-60,CH-47F	General Support Aviation Battalion
638th Aviation Support Battalion		Ground Support Unit
40th Combat Aviation Brigade (40th Infantry Division)		
Headquarters and Headquarters Company (Stockton, California)		
1st Battalion, 211th Aviation Regiment	AH-64E	Attack/Reconnaissance Battalion
1st Battalion, 140th Aviation Regiment	UH-60	Assault Battalion
1st Battalion, 168th Aviation Regiment	UH-60,CH-47F	General Support Aviation Battalion
3rd Battalion, 140th Aviation Regiment	UH-60, UH-72	Security & Support Battalion
1st Battalion, 126th Aviation Regiment	UH-60, CH-47F	General Support Aviation Battalion
640th Aviation Support Battalion		Ground Support Unit
42nd Combat Aviation Brigade (42nd Infantry Division)		
Headquarters and Headquarters Company (Latham, New York)		
1st Battalion, 151st Aviation Regiment	AH-64E	Attack/Reconnaissance Battalion
3rd Battalion, 142nd Aviation Regiment	UH-60	Assault Battalion
1st Battalion, 171st Aviation Regiment	UH-60,CH-47F	General Support Aviation Battalion
1st Battalion, 224th Aviation Regiment	UH-60, UH-72	Security & Support Battalion
642nd Aviation Support Battalion		Ground Support Unit

deployed to Iraq and Syria in 2017 for Operation Inherent Resolve.

From its headquarters in Kinston in North Carolina, the 449th Combat Aviation Brigade controls aviation units spread across southwestern states, including the only attack helicopter battalion assigned to a separate aviation brigade. The brigade traces its roots to 1987 when it was formed as an ARNG aviation group for the XVIII Airborne Corps. In 2006, it was expanded to become a theatre aviation brigade, given a support and communications mission. During 2018, it deployed to the Middle East for Operation Inherent Resolve. It was re-organised as a combat aviation brigade in 2021, and its attack helicopter battalion was converted to the upgraded Boeing AH-64E Apache in 2023.

ABOVE: California Army National Guard aviators from 1st Battalion, 126th Aviation Regiment, practise firefighting techniques with the California Department of Forestry and Fire Protection. (US ARMY NATIONAL GUARD, STAFF SGT EDDIE SIGUENZA)

ABOVE: Minnesota National Guard aviators return home after completing a nine-month deployment to Bogotá, Columbia, where they supported the United States Southern Command's Combat Transnational Organized Crime Counter-Drug and Counter-Narcotics mission in April 2024 with C-12 Huron flight operations, transporting passengers and cargo throughout South America. (MINNESOTA NATIONAL GUARD, SGT 1ST CLASS BEN HOUTKOOPER)

Army National Guard Separate Aviation Brigades

63rd Theatre Aviation Brigade		
Headquarters and Headquarters Company (Frankfort, Kentucky)		
1st Battalion, 108th Aviation Regiment	UH-60M	Assault Battalion
2nd Battalion, 135th Aviation Regiment	UH-60, CH-47F	General Support Aviation Battalion
1st Battalion, 376th Aviation Regiment	UH-60, UH-72	Security & Support Battalion
498th Aviation Support Battalion		Ground Support Unit
77th Expeditionary Combat Aviation Brigade		
Headquarters and Headquarters Company (Little Rock, Arkansas)		
1st Battalion, 114th Aviation Regiment	UH-60, UH-72	Security & Support Battalion
777th Aviation Support Battalion		Ground Support Unit
185th Aviation Brigade		
Headquarters and Headquarters Company (Jackson, Missouri)		
1st Battalion, 185th Aviation Regiment	UH-60, CH-47F	Assault Battalion
1st Battalion, 111th Aviation Regiment	UH-60, CH-47F	General Support Aviation Battalion
449th Combat Aviation Brigade		
Headquarters and Headquarters Company (Kinton, North Carolina)		
1st Battalion, 130th Aviation Regiment	AH-64E	Attack/Reconnaissance Battalion
1st Battalion, 131st Aviation Regiment	UH-60	Assault Battalion

Reserve Aviators

Providing critical combat support

The United States Army Reserve (USAR) force comprised some 175,424 soldiers and 12,200 civilian staff in 2024. It has units in all 50 states and five US territories, as well as in Germany, Korea and Japan, supporting its active-duty colleagues.

It is a cost-efficient force that provides a ready reserve of trained personnel who can be rapidly mobilised to support the active-duty US Army, contributing 16% of the total force but only costing 6% of its total budget.

The USAR was formed in 1916 to provide the regular army and National Guard with a pool of reserve personnel who could be mobilised in time of war. As a branch of the federal armed forces, the USAR is under the direct control of the US Army and is organised and equipped to augment it in time of crisis or war.

Unlike the ARNG, which assigns its aviation to specific divisions, the USAR is configured to provide specialist combat service support roles, such as communications, medical, engineering, military police and legal. It has a mix of specialist brigades, regiments, battalions and smaller detachments that are trained and equipped to reinforce or augment larger formations of the active-duty army.

This concept is central to how the US Army Reserve Aviation Command operates and deploys to overseas combat zones. Its headquarters commands all aviation assets in the USAR and co-ordinates all their peacetime training. It is located at Fort Knox, Kentucky, and is commanded by a brigadier general.

A significant proportion of USAR personnel are former active-duty soldiers and they take their experience and skills with them into their reserve duty. USAR aviation units usually train or drill one weekend a month and are activated for a two-week training period each year. Personnel also regularly undergo longer training courses to enhance their skills. Each unit contains a full-time cadre of training and administrative personnel.

ABOVE: Army Reserve CH-47 Chinook crews practise under-slinging loads during an ammunition supply exercise at Sparta-Fort McCoy Airport in Wisconsin. (US ARMY, SCOTT T STURKOL)

RIGHT: Reserve soldiers from the 11th Combat Aviation Brigade and Israeli Air Force UH-60 Black Hawk helicopters in formation with a US Presidential Airlift Group VH-60 helicopter during a rehearsal in Israel in 2022 ahead of US President Joe Biden's visit to the Middle East country. (US ARMY)

US Army Reserve Aviation Command

	Location	Helicopters/Aircraft	Unit Role
11th Expeditionary Combat Aviation Brigade			
Headquarters and Headquarters Company	Fort Carson, Colorado		
1st Battalion, 158th Aviation Regiment	Spring, Texas	30 × UH-60L	Assault Battalion
7th Battalion, 158th Aviation Regiment	Fort Hood, Texas	8 × UH-60L, 15 × HH-60M, 12 × CH-47F	General Support Aviation Battalion
6th Battalion, 52nd Aviation Regiment	Los Alamitos, California	4 × C-12F, 4 × CV-12VF, 8 × UC-35A	Theater Fixed Wing Battalion
90th Aviation Support Battalion	Fort Worth, Texas		Ground Support Unit
244th Expeditionary Combat Aviation Brigade			
Headquarters and Headquarters Company	Fort Knox, Kentucky		
8th Battalion, 229th Aviation Regiment	Fort Knox, Kentucky	30 × UH-60L	Assault Battalion
5th Battalion, 159th Aviation Regiment	Fort Eustis, Virginia	23 × UH-60L, 15 × HH-60M, 12 × CH-47F	General Support Aviation Battalion
2nd Battalion, 228th Aviation Regiment	Joint Base McGuire–Dix–Lakehurst , New Jersey	24 × C-12F, 8 × UC-35A	Theater Fixed Wing Battalion

LEFT: USAR CH-47 Chinooks from the 5th Battalion, 159th Aviation Regiment, were moved by ship to Rota naval base in Spain ahead of the Defender 2023 exercises to test the rapid reinforcement of NATO. (US ARMY RESERVE, NATALIE WEAVER)

BELOW: Assault training with the 101st Airborne Division (Air Assault) is regularly carried out by the USAR's 8th Battalion, 229th Aviation Regiment, as part of its role to augment active-duty aviation units. (US ARMY, MASTER SGT MARK BELL)

ABOVE: A USAR UH-60 flew a casualty evacuation mission to lift a US soldier injured during a NATO training exercise to Linköping University Hospital in Sweden in May **2024.** (US ARMY RESERVE)

RIGHT: UH-60s flown by the USAR 11th Theater Aviation Command (now 11th Expeditionary Combat Aviation Brigade) conducted medical evacuation training with soldiers from the 19th Engineer Battalion in Fort Knox, Kentucky, in 2016. (US ARMY RESERVE, KEVIN COATES)

As well as its overseas operations role, the command is also tasked to support the Federal Emergency Management Agency (FEMA) within the continental United States when responding to emergencies.

In its current form, the command was activated in September 2016 with its main units and personnel grouped into two expeditionary combat aviation brigades. The command currently comprises 4,400 soldiers supported by 600 civilian staff, and flies around 200 fixed-wing aircraft and helicopters, based across 12 states.

Its units specialise in providing air assault, air movement, air traffic services, airfield management, aeromedical evacuation, combat aviation brigade reinforcement, theatre aviation support and co-ordination of aviation staging and onward movement to operational theatres. It currently operates Sikorsky UH-60 Black Hawk, Boeing CH-47F Chinook, Beechcraft C-12 Heron and Cessna Citation V (UC-35) platforms.

In line with the increasing specialisation of support roles, the USAR stood down its last McDonnell Douglas AH-64D Apache in March 2015, when the 1st Battalion, the 158tht Aviation Regiment traded its attack helicopters for UH-60s.

The command traces its history back to the 11th Aviation Group, activated in 1963 to be the aviation unit of the experimental 11th Air Assault Division (Test) under the command of airmobile pioneer Brigadier General Harry Kinnard. In July 1965, the division was reflagged as the 1st Cavalry Division (Airmobile) before it deployed to Vietnam as the first-ever airmobile formation to see battle. After nearly 20 years based in Germany, the group was de-activated as an active-duty unit and then reformed in 2005 as the 11th Theatre Aviation Command at Fort Knox, to control all USAR reserve units,

USAR's two expeditionary combat air brigades are configured as theatre support formations, which when deployed provide lines of communications support in operational theatres. They each have an assault aviation battalion with UH-60s, a general support aviation battalion with CH-47Fs

ABOVE: The 7th Battalion, 158th Aviation Regiment flown by reserve aviators provided medical evacuation support for US and allied units across the Middle East with UH-60 Black Hawks during Operation Inherent Resolve deployment in 2022. (US ARMY RESERVE)

USAR UH-60 Black Hawk Helicopters from the 8th Battalion, 229th Aviation Regiment, based at Fort Knox, regularly train with their active-duty colleagues from the 101st Airborne Division (Air Assault). (US ARMY RESERVE, SGT STEPHANIE RAMIREZ)

ABOVE: The USAR retired its last AH-64D in March 2016 during a ceremony at Conroe in Texas. (US ARMY, CAPT MATTHEW ROMAN)

and UH-60s, as well as a theatre fixed-wing battalion with C-12s and UC-35 aircraft. Their missions include air mobility, aeromedical evacuation, reconnaissance and logistical support.

The 11th Expeditionary Combat Aviation Brigade, headquartered at Fort Carson in Colorado, was formed in 2016 to take command of three USAR aviation battalions.

The other USAR reserve formation, the 244th Expeditionary Combat Aviation Brigade, is headquartered at Fort Knox. It has a similar structure to the 11th Brigade, controlling more than 1,850 soldiers and around 110 helicopters and other aircraft, based in seven states.

The 244th Brigade has always been a reserve formation since its origin in 1988; it moved to Fort Knox in 2020.

On mobilisation, the 244th Expeditionary Combat Aviation Brigade (ECAB) is deployed to provide operational aviation support to the US Army and joint forces. The brigade's diverse capabilities enable it to conduct aviation operations in both combat and humanitarian environments, ensuring the delivery of personnel, equipment and supplies to where they are needed most.

Both of the USAR brigade headquarters are modular organisations that are configured to bring under command a range of activity duty and reserve component aviation units. In 2019, the 244th Brigade deployed to Kuwait and Iraq to take command of all US Army aviation units, both active-duty and reserve, taking part in Operation Inherent Resolve. These units

BELOW: USAR CH-47 Chinook helicopters with the 7th General Support Aviation Brigade deployed to the Middle East for Operation Inherent Resolve in 2022. (US ARMY, SGT STEVEN LEWIS)

operated across Iraq, Syria and Jordan in the fight against the Islamic State insurgent group as Task Force Warhawk.

The brigade headquarters deployed to Iraq for a year and took under command several aviation units as they rotated in and out of the theatre. Its aviators operated across the Middle East, supporting US and allied troops in complex combat actions. An additional role for the brigade was to help train Iraqi army aviators so they could step up to help in the fight against the Islamic State.

In 2022, it was the turn of the 11th Brigade to deploy to the Middle East for Operation Inherent Resolve duty, as Task Force Eagle. Just like the 244th Brigade, the 11th Brigade took under command several active-duty and reserve units to operate across Syria, Iraq and Jordan.

ABOVE: Aviators from the Army Reserve Aviation Command assisted in transferring the remains of US soldiers from the 1846-48 Mexican-American War, from Monterrey in Mexico to Dover Air Force Base, Delaware, for a ceremony led by the US Army's Old Guard. (US ARMY RESERVE, CAPT MATTHEW ROMAN)

LEFT: UC-35A Citation 560 executive jets serve in the USAR Aviation Command to rapidly move VIPs and priority cargo around operational theatres. (ADRIAN PINGSTONE)

Boeing AH-64E Apache

Improving the Apache

RIGHT: An AH-64 Apache conducting snow operations certification training at Fort Wainwright in Alaska. (US ARMY)

The first generation of armed helicopters developed in the 1950s and 1960s were simply transport or observation platforms that had weapons strapped on their fuselage. This was a quick and easy way to field aerial firepower, but these first gunships were far from ideal.

It was not until the famous Bell AH-1 Cobra took to the skies in the late 1960s that purpose-built attack helicopters saw action. The Cobra used the engine, transmission and tail section of the classic UH-1 'Huey', but did away with its troop-carrying compartment, which reduced weight and enhanced manoeuvrability. Its pilot and gunner sat in a tandem configuration at the front of the helicopter to give them a superb view of the battlefield. Small stub wings were stacked with rockets and guns and a rotating turret under the nose contained a mini-gun or grenade launchers.

The instant success of the Cobra in Vietnam saw other nations move to field their own dedicated attack helicopters and the US Army soon set to work improving the Cobra. This coincided with rapid developments in anti-tank guided weapons in the 1960s and it became possible to employ them from helicopters, creating flying tank killers.

After several false starts to build a new tank-killing attack helicopter, the Hughes Aircraft Company was selected to build the YAH-64 in 1976. Five years later, the first-production Apache was handed over to the US Army to begin operational testing. It entered full-scale production as the AH-64A in 1982 and by the end of the decade more than 500 were in service.

The 1970s and 1980s saw rapid advances in the development of

BELOW: Two AH-64 Apaches in Australia for Exercise Talisman Sabre 2019 to demonstrate the attack helicopters to potential opponents in the Pacific region. (US ARMY)

BOEING AH-64E APACHE

Powerplant:	2 × T700-GE-701D engines
Length:	17.7m (58ft)
Height:	5m (16ft 4in)
Maximum take-off weight:	10,432kg (23,000lb)
Maximum level flight speed:	276 kph (149 knots)
Range:	476km (257 miles)
Crew:	2
Armament	
Guns:	M230 Chain Gun, 1200 rounds
Missiles:	AGM-114 Hellfire, Joint Air-to-Ground Missile (JAGM)
Rockets:	Hydra 70

allow the crew to access and share information rapidly with ground forces and other aircraft, including the facility for the AH-64E crew to control unmanned aerial vehicles flying as part of joint missions. A maritime mode is provided to enhance the performance of the Longbow radar when operating over water. Embedded system-level diagnostics are incorporated in the new helicopter to allow ground crews to rapidly assess maintenance requirements between missions.

The first deliveries of pre-production helicopters began in November 2011. Test flights went well and full-rate production was approved by the US Army in October 2012, ➲

ABOVE: An AH-64E Apache from 1st Battalion, 25th Aviation Regiment, takes off from its landing pad after arming and refuelling during the unit's rotation at the National Training Center, Fort Irwin, California. (US ARMY)

BELOW: The APG-78 Longbow millimetre-wave fire-control radar allows the AH-64D/E Apache to find and identify targets at night or in bad weather. (HUNINI)

sensor technology and soon this was incorporated on the Apache. Thermal imaging sensors allowed AH-64 crews to spot targets at long range at night, with computer technology being used to 'slave' sensors to weapon sights to allow rapid and accurate target engagement. Thanks to its powerful night-vision sensors, the Apache devastated Iraq tank divisions during the brief land phase of Operation Desert Storm in February 1991.

Battlefield radars were now being developed that were small enough to be installed on attack helicopters. This led to the Longbow radar being mounted on a disc above the rotor hub of the AH-64D variant of the McDonnell Douglas AH-64D Apache Longbow. This allowed the crew to identify and target the enemy in fog and rain that would normally impact the performance of thermal imaging sensors.

The latest variant of the iconic Apache features improved weapons, sensors and engines to make it more lethal and survivable on the battlefields of the future. Initially known as the AH-64D Block III, in 2012 it was formerly redesignated as the Boeing AH-64E

Guardian and was quickly dubbed by its crews the '64 Echo.

US Army aviation commanders wanted to enhance the Apache's combat performance by giving it new and more powerful engines and making it easier for crews to share battlefield information with fixed-wing strike aircraft, helicopters and ground forces. They also wanted to field modern avionics and software-driven mission systems to allow new sensors and weapons to be easily and cheaply integrated on to the AH-64E.

The new helicopter featured improved digital connectivity, via the Joint Tactical Information Distribution System, more powerful T700-GE-701D engines with upgraded face gear transmission to handle more power, capability to control unmanned aerial vehicles (UAVs) and improved landing gear. New composite rotor blades, increased cruise speed, climb rate and payload capacity allow the AH-64E to fly faster and further.

At the heart of the enhancements are new avionics and digital communications via a Joint Tactical Information Distribution System to

ABOVE: A defensive aid suite of decoy flares protects the AH-64 Apache from heat-seeking missile threats. (OFFICE OF THE PRESIDENT OF TAIWAN)

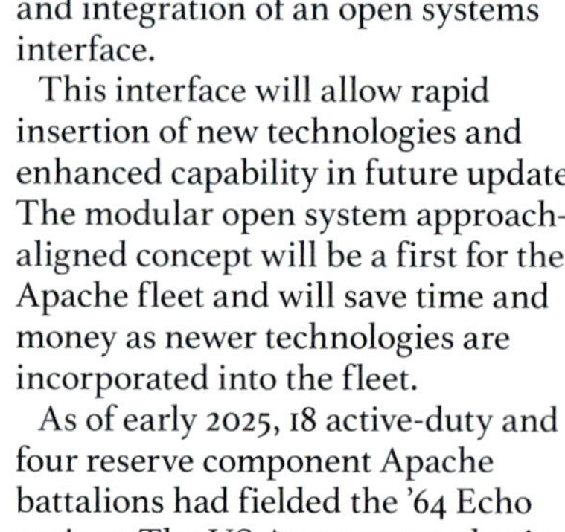

with plans for the service's 634 AH-64Ds to be upgraded to AH-64E standard. The US Army contracted Boeing to build new airframes and to remanufacture old D models into the new configuration by re-using fuselages and other components.

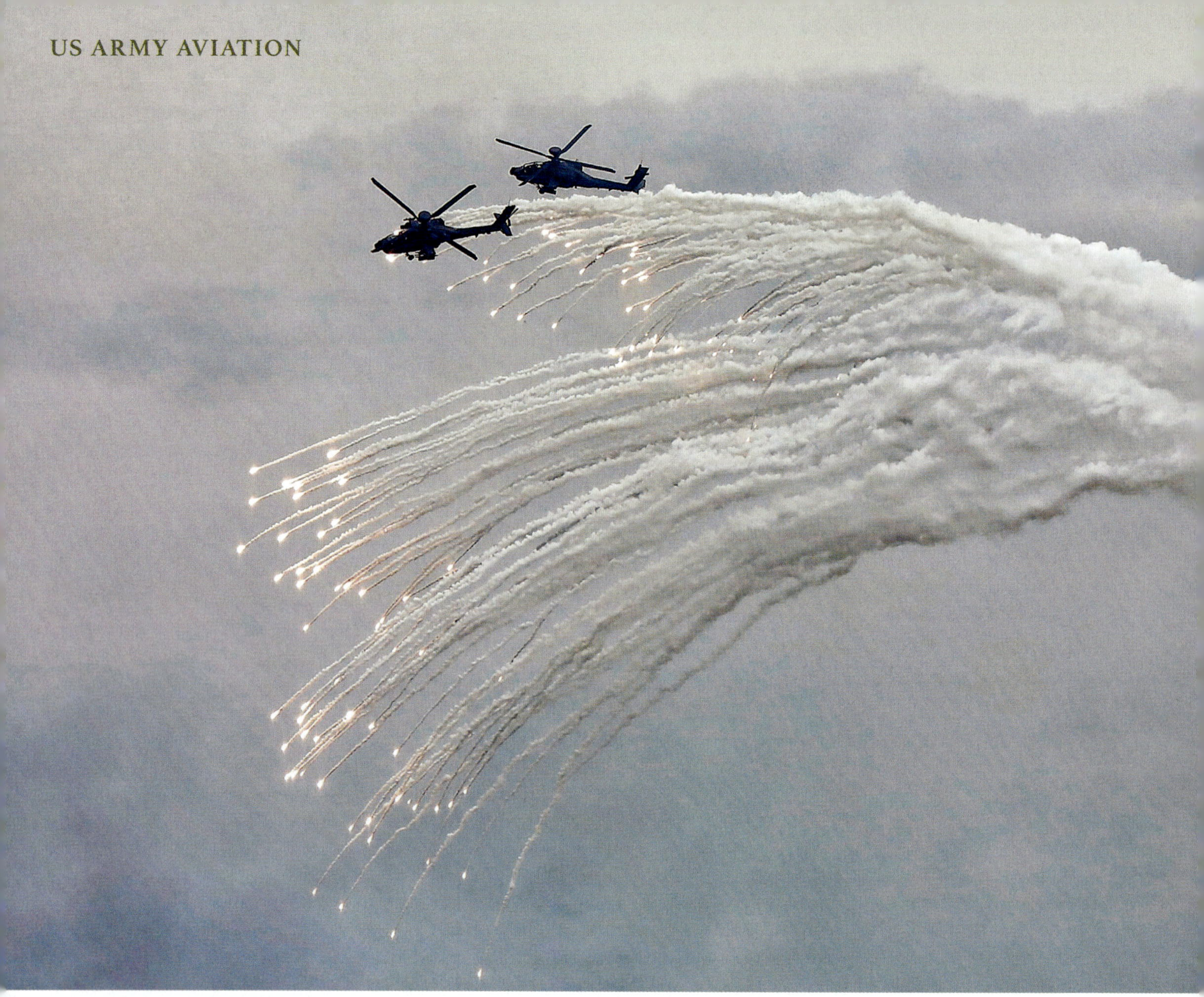

In November 2013, the AH-64E achieved initial operating capability and five months later the 1st Battalion, 229th Attack Reconnaissance Regiment deployed with its 24 AH-64Es to Afghanistan in the type's first combat deployment. The AH-64E has since gone through several iterations for US and overseas customers.

The newest V6.5 version of the AH-64E Apache successfully flew in Mesa, Arizona, on October 11, 2023. This version includes software updates enhancing capabilities and improving the pilot interface. Some of those enhancements include optimised route and attack planning, enhanced Link 16 datalink features and integration of an open systems interface.

This interface will allow rapid insertion of new technologies and enhanced capability in future updates. The modular open system approach-aligned concept will be a first for the Apache fleet and will save time and money as newer technologies are incorporated into the fleet.

As of early 2025, 18 active-duty and four reserve component Apache battalions had fielded the '64 Echo variant. The US Army currently aims to buy 678 AH-64E and continues to fund the purchase of new-build and remanufacture of old helicopters. In May 2025, US Defense Secretary Pete Hegseth announced plans to accelerate the retirement of the AH-64D and rapidly move to an all '64 Echo fleet.

RIGHT: The US Army regularly embarks AH-64 Apache attack helicopters on US Navy amphibious ships as part of their preparation for littoral operations. (US NAVY)

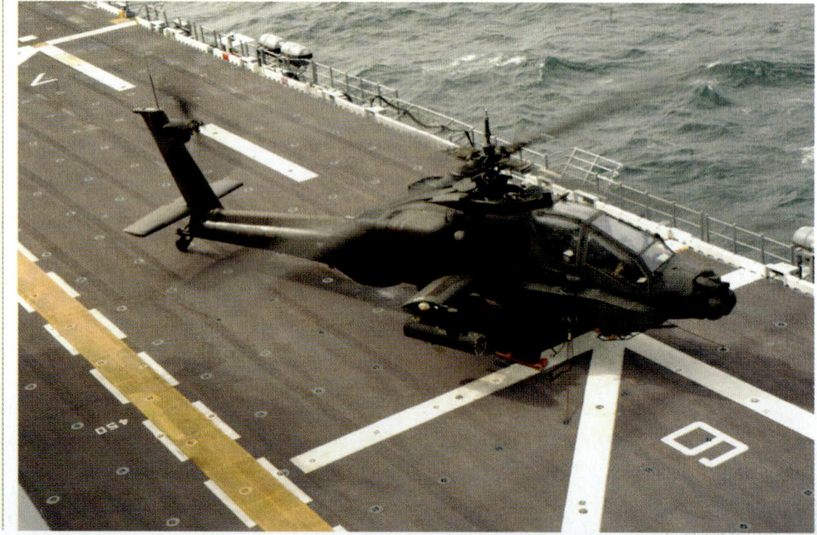

ABOVE: The Apache AH 64E packs tremendous firepower, with Hellfire missiles, Hydra rockets and its 30mm chain gun. (BOEING)

LEFT: The AH-64E is the latest variant of the Apache family of attack helicopters and features advance avionics, computer software and weapons options. (US ARMY)

ABOVE: NASA used the Boeing CH-47B to support the US space programme in the 1980s. (NASA)

CH-47 Chinook

Heavy Lift for the US Army

When American soldiers need moving quickly around a battlefield, want an urgent re-supply of ammunition or relocation to a safer position, they call for a Boeing CH-47 Chinook. As they hear the approaching sound of the big helicopter, they know their problems are solved, for today.

America soldiers in Vietnam soon nicknamed the Chinook 'Big Windy', on account of the large amount of downwash it generated. The name stuck and is still used to this day.

Nothing is quite like the Chinook. It can lift more than ten tons of cargo and carry up to 55 troops, thanks to its two Lycoming T55 turboshaft engines. Crucially, the engines have been constantly upgraded since the 1960s, ensuring it had superb hot-high performance in the jungles of Vietnam or the mountains of Afghanistan.

The counter-rotating rotors mean it does not need an anti-torque vertical tail rotor, so all the power from the engines can be used to lift cargo or to power forward flight. It also makes the Chinook very stable, allowing crews to accurately position underslung loads in delicate situations.

The unique design of the Chinook can be traced back to the tandem rotor concepts pioneered by early designer Frank Piasecki, who began building helicopters in Morton in Pennsylvania in the mid-1940s. His PV-3, later known as the HRP-1, was the first US military helicopter that could carry significant cargo and passengers. The Piasecki Helicopter Corporation was renamed Vertol Corporation in early 1956. Four years later, the company was acquired by Boeing in 1960 and renamed Boeing Vertol. It became the Boeing Helicopter Division

RIGHT: Hovering with only the rear wheels touching the edge of a cliff, a 1st Cavalry Division CH-47F prepares to offload troops. The pinnacle manoeuvre allows the pilots to drop off ground forces in areas too dangerous or too difficult for a full landing. (US ARMY)

in 1987. The company still makes helicopters, including the Chinook, in Pennsylvania.

On September 21, 1961, test pilots of what was then the Boeing Vertol company lifted the YCH-1B prototype off the ground for the first time. A year later, in line with the US Army's policy of naming its helicopters after Native American tribes, the machine honoured the Chinook people of the US Pacific Northwest. During 1962, the HC-1B was redesignated the CH-47A under the new United States Tri-Service aircraft designation system.

Three years later, the first Chinooks were heading to South Vietnam with the iconic airmobile unit, the 1st Cavalry Division. The rest, as they say, is history. Over the following 60 years the Chinook has remained the US Army's main heavy-lift helicopter, and has seen action in every American war since. The helicopter has been progressively updated, with new engines, avionics, armament and defensive systems.

Currently, the CH-47F Block I variant is in service across US Army general support aviation battalions. The prototype Foxtrot variant made its maiden flight in 2001, and the first production model rolled out at Boeing's facility in Ridley Park, Pennsylvania, and first flew in October 2006.

Improvements included 4,868-shaft-horsepower (3,630kW) Honeywell engines and an airframe with better integrated construction for lower maintenance requirements. New construction techniques reduced vibration, as well as inspection and repair needs, and eliminated flexing points to increase service life. Its avionics have been improved by the installation of a Rockwell Collins Common Avionics Architecture ❯

ABOVE: CH-47A Chinooks first saw combat in Vietnam with the 1st Cavalry Division (Airmobile). (US ARMY)

LEFT: CH-4F model Chinooks are powered by the Lycoming T55-GA-714A turboshaft engine. (MR.Z-MAN)

ABOVE: Generations of US soldiers have come to love the 'Big Windy' for its power, speed and comfort. (US ARMY)

BELOW: 101st Airborne Division (Air Assault) troops prepare to board CH-47s during the war in Afghanistan. The Chinook's power enabled it to operate in the hot-high conditions in the central Asian country. (US ARMY)

CH-47F BLOCK I CHINOOK	
Power plant:	2 × Textron Lycoming T55-4-714 turboshafts
Length:	15.87m (52ft 1in)
Height:	5.59m (18ft 4in)
Max take-off weight:	24,494kg (54,000lb)
Max speed:	259km/h (161mph)
Range:	1,382km (746nm)
Crew:	5
Armament	
2 × M134 7.62mm miniguns (front)	
2 × M240D 7.62mm machine gun (rear)	

System cockpit, and a BAE Systems' Digital Advanced Flight Control System (DAFCS).

The first CH-47Fs were delivered to the US Army by August 2008 and by 2025 all of the active-duty US Army, Army National Guard and US Army Reserve Chinook fleet comprises Block I Foxtrot models. The CH-47F Block II entered the production phase in April 2022 and the first upgraded helicopter was delivered to the US Army in July 2024.

The new Block II helicopter boasts an improved drive train, redesigned fuel tanks and a more robust fuselage to deliver enhanced lift and mission radius. It has a Max Gross Weight of 54,000lbs – an increase of 4,000lbs on the Block I – and can carry payloads up to 22,000lbs, while its upgraded Honeywell T55-714C engines are 20% more powerful than its predecessor.

The iconic CH-47 Chinook heavy-lift helicopter plays a central role in the US Army's 160th Special Operations Aviation Regiment (Airborne), or SOAR(A). In the 1980s, 12 Chinooks were modified for special operations missions. Six C and six D models were fitted with in-flight refuelling, a fast rope-rappelling system, enhanced defensive systems and communications upgrades. These helicopters saw service in Operation Desert Storm in 1991.

An improved version, the MH-47E, was ordered in 1991 and featured more powerful engines, increased fuel capacity and terrain-following, terrain-avoidance radar. During the 1990s, 26 MH-46Es were delivered to the 2nd Battalion of the 160th SOAR(A). This was the version that bore the brunt of operations in Afghanistan from 2001 onwards.

The huge demand for special operations aviation to fight the 'Global War on Terrorism' after 2001 led the US Army to order an upgraded model, the MH-47G. Improvements included more powerful engines, an easier to maintain fuselage and sophisticated avionics based around the digital Common Avionics Architecture System (CAAS). As a result, the MH-47G could fly faster for longer, and can operate longer before requiring major overhauls.

The US Army ordered the conversion of the surviving 25 MH-47Es and 11 MH-47Ds to the new G model configuration, with work to be completed by 2003. In 2002, plans to expand the 160th Regiment were announced and 12 extra MH-60Gs were ordered to be delivered by 2011.

In September 2020, the US Army ordered a batch of 24 helicopters to be built to a new standard, dubbed the MH-47G Block II. These new-build helicopters incorporate many of the improvements that feature in the

CH-47F Block II variant, including a comprehensive defensive aids suite and low-level/adverse weather piloting aids, such as forward-looking infrared and multi-mode/terrain-following radar. It is armed with two 7.62mm M134 miniguns and two M240 7.62mm machine guns. It is

eventually intended that US Army Special Operations Command will have a fleet of 69 MH-47G Block II helicopters.

The mighty Chinook looks set to soldier on in US Army service beyond 2060, more than 100 years after the first one entered service.

ABOVE: 21st century Chinooks boast 'glass-cockpit' displays to help pilots better monitor huge quantities of flight and tactical information. (US ARMY, SGT MICHAEL WILSON)

The Chinook has proved an export success for Boeing with several NATO allies, including Canada, Greece, UK, Italy, Spain, Turkey and the Netherlands, operating the heavy-lift helicopter. (PAUL TOLENAAR)

UH-60

The Black Hawk

RIGHT: Generations of UH-60 Black Hawk pilots have flown the helicopter in environments ranging from jungles, deserts, mountains and the frozen **Arctic.** (NEW YORK ARMY NATIONAL GUARD, 1ST LT JEAN MARIE KRATZER)

BELOW: The UH-60 Black Hawk has provided stalwart service in all of America's wars since the 1983 invasion of Grenada, including prolonged deployments in the **Middle East.** (US NAVY, CHIEF PHOTOGRAPHER'S MATE EDWARD G MARTENS)

Thanks to the book and Hollywood movie, *Black Hawk Down*, the classic helicopter is forever associated with US Army aviation. The Sikorsky UH-60 Black Hawk first entered service with the US Army in 1979.

Its speed, capacity and flexibility has made the Black Hawk indispensable to the US Army; UH-60 crews love the helicopter for its reliability and ability to take fire during combat missions.

The US Army uses the Black Hawk primarily as an air assault helicopter to deliver troops onto the battlefield, in all weathers and environments. Crews are trained in low-level flying at night in bad weather and dropping off their passengers in a few seconds. Every US Army combat aviation brigade has an assault battalion with 30 UH-60s, which allows it to transport a battalion of air assault infantry in one lift.

Black Hawks have seen action in every US military campaign since the 1983 invasion of Grenada. The biggest test of the UH-60 was during the 1991 Gulf War when more than 300 Black Hawks carried the 101st and 82nd Airborne Divisions deep into Iraq to outflank Saddam Hussein's troops occupying Kuwait.

The UH-60 is expected to be in service for many decades to come. Just over 2,000 remain in service with the US Army and new variants continue to be manufactured.

During more than four decades of US military service, the helicopter has progressively upgraded its UH-60 variants with new engines, avionics, engines, transmissions and structures. The US Army has gone through the A, L, M and V models.

The prototype YUH-60A made its first flight in October 1974 and three years later the original UH-60A US Army version entered production. The Alpha model had a crew of four and could carry up to 11 equipped troops. It had two T700-GE-700 engines. Up to 1989, a total of 1,048 UH-60As had been built for the US Army. From 1989 until 2007, the army upgraded all its UH-60As to L standard with enhanced T700-GE-701C engines, an improved durability gearbox and updated flight control systems. Further upgrades led to GE T700-GE-701D engines being installed in UH-60Ls.

At the start of the 21st century, the US Army launched its next version of the Black Hawk, which was dubbed the UH-60M. This included improved wide chord rotor blades, more powerful T700-GE-701D engines, improved durability gearbox, Integrated Vehicle Health Management System computer and new Common Avionics Architecture System (CAAS) 'glass cockpit'.

The first of 22 new UH-60Ms was delivered in July 2006 and a year later full-rate production of ➤

ABOVE: Air assault is the primary mission of the UH-60 Black Hawk, delivering US troops far behind enemy lines to cause surprise and disruption to enemies. (US ARMY)

SIKORSKY UH-60M BLACK HAWK

Power Plant:	2 × General Electric T700-GE-700Ds
Length:	17.1m (64ft 8in)
Height:	4.4m (16ft 8in)
Maximum take-off weight:	9,900kg (22,000lb)
Speed:	269kph (184mph)
Range:	933km (504nm)
Crew:	4
Armament	
2 × 7.62mm or .50 cal machine guns	

LEFT: Sikorsky's YUH-60A (front) when head-to-head with Boeing Vertol YUH-61A (rear) in a fly-off in the 1970s to win the US Army's competition for its next-generation air assault helicopter. (US ARMY)

Fuel tanks and weapons can be carried on stub-wing pylons to extend mission options for UH-60 Black Hawk commanders. Extending range and endurance is particularly important during casualty evacuation missions. (US ARMY, CHIEF MASS COMMUNICATIONS SPECIALIST GREG BINGAMAN)

It saw action in the Arabian Gulf and Operation Desert Storm. The helicopter featured additional avionics, night-vision-capable cockpit, a thermal imaging turret, M134 door guns, internal auxiliary fuel tanks and other special operations mission equipment.

During the late 1980s, the 160th Regiment began to look to field a more capable helicopter to replace its MH-60As. It ordered the MH-60K in 1988, which had air-to-air refuelling, T700-GE-701C engines, an integrated glass cockpit, AN/APQ-174B terrain-following radar, colour weather map, improved weapons capability and better defensive systems. As an interim until the MH-60K was ready for the service, the 160th Regiment took delivery of 37 MH-60Ls during the 1990s. These had many of the improvements to be fielded in the K model, but only ten were eventually fitted for air-to-air refuelling.

The 160th Regiment is the sole operator of the MH-60L Direct Action Penetrator (DAP) variant. It is configured as a gunship, with no troop-carrying capacity. The helicopter is equipped with stub wings, each capable of carrying configurations of the M230 chain gun 30mm automatic cannon, 19-shot Hydra 70 rocket pod, AGM-114 Hellfire missiles, AIM-92 Stinger air-to-air missiles, GAU-19 gun pods and M134 minigun pods. M134D miniguns are used as door guns. In 2011, a major programme to upgrade all special operations Black Hawks began to be modernised to MH-60M configuration.

1,227 helicopters was authorised. Production of the Mike version continues today.

The UH-60V is an upgraded version of the UH-60L, which incorporates the glass cockpit used on the UH-60M. Northrop Grumman and KBR received the first contract in 2022 to begin modifying Lima model helicopters for use by the Army National Guard.

Under current plans, the US Army is continuing to buy new-build Mike model Black Hawks and rebuilt Limas into Victor models. The US Army's Acquisition Objective is for a total of 2,135, which will include a combination 1,367 UH-60M and 760 UH-60V conversion models.

The UH-60 was soon adopted by the 160th Special Operations Aviation Regiment (Airborne) – SOAR (A). Special operations aviators have prized the Black Hawk because of its speed and reliability in extreme environments.

Special operations variants of the helicopter have also been progressively modified to incorporate the improvements made in the wider UH-60 fleet.

The first modified Black Hawk operated by the 160th Regiment was the MH-60A and 30 helicopters were converted to this configuration.

MH-6 Little Bird

Go Fast, Go Low

The US Army's 160th Special Operations Aviation Regiment (Airborne) – SOAR(A) – is the sole user of a fleet of light attack helicopters modified for highly dangerous missions behind enemy lines.

In the 1960s, the reclusive entrepreneur and inventor Howard Hughes sold the US Army a version of his high-speed and highly agile Model 369 light helicopter. This became famous in the Vietnam War as the OH-6 Cayuse, but it was soon nicknamed by the Air Cavalry as the 'Loach' after the US Army requirement acronym LOH – light observation helicopter.

When the US Army formed the 160th SOAR(A) in the aftermath of the Desert One debacle in Iran in 1980, it turned to the OH-6 as a gunship to support special operations missions. Compared with the big Black Hawks and Chinooks on the ramp at Fort Campbell in Kentucky, the OH-6 looked ridiculously small, so they were soon nicknamed 'Little Birds'. The name stuck.

Since then, the 160th SOAR(A) has progressively upgraded its Little Birds. A dedicated attack variant is dubbed the AH-6 and a special operations variant, the MH-6, is optimised to move small groups of troops. The AH/MH-6 fleet has been upgraded to J standard with improved engines, avionics, navigation systems and night-vision sensors.

ABOVE: The AH/MH-6 has been progressively upgraded over the past 40 years and the latest version, the J model, features advanced avionics and night-vision sensors. (US ARMY)

MH-6 LITTLE BIRD	
Powerplant: 1 × Allison T63-A-5A or T63-A-700 turboshafts	
Length: 7.50m (24ft 7.2in)	
Width: 1.402m (4ft 7.2in)	
Height: 2.67m (8ft 9in)	
Maximum take-off weight: 3,100lb (1,406kg)	
Speed: 282kph (175mph)	
Range: 430km (232 miles)	
Crew: 2	
Capacity: up to 6 passengers	
Armament	
2 × 12.7×99mm (.50 BMG) GAU-19; or 2 × 7.62×51mm NATO M134 minigun	
2 × LAU-68D/A 7-tube rocket pods firing 2.75in (70 mm) Hydra 70 rocket projectiles	
4 × AGM-114 Hellfire air-to-ground missiles or 4 × FIM-92 Stinger air-to-air missiles	

BELOW: AH-6 Little Birds played an important role in the 2003 invasion of Iraq, leading the advance of US Special Operations Forces across its western desert. (US DOD/COMBAT CAMERA)

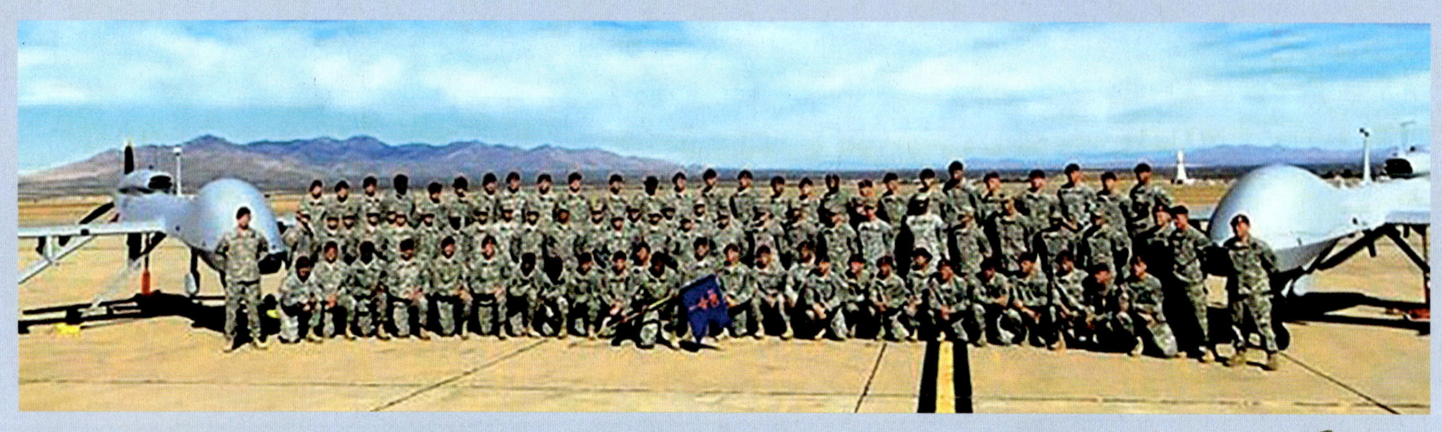

MQ-1C Gray Eagle

The US Army's Universal Drone

ABOVE: US Army's Special Operations Aviation units have their own derivatives of the famous Predator drone, known as MQ-1C Gray Eagle. (US ARMY)

RIGHT: Civilian contactors from General Atomics load Hellfire missiles onto an MQ-1C Gray Eagle at Camp Taji in Iraq in February 2011, during one of the drone's first operational deployments. (US ARMY)

BELOW: An MQ-1C Gray Eagle takes off from Ladd Army Airfield at Fort Wainwright, Alaska, in 2016, a year after the UAV was first deployed to the 49th State. (US ARMY, STAFF SGT SEAN BRADY)

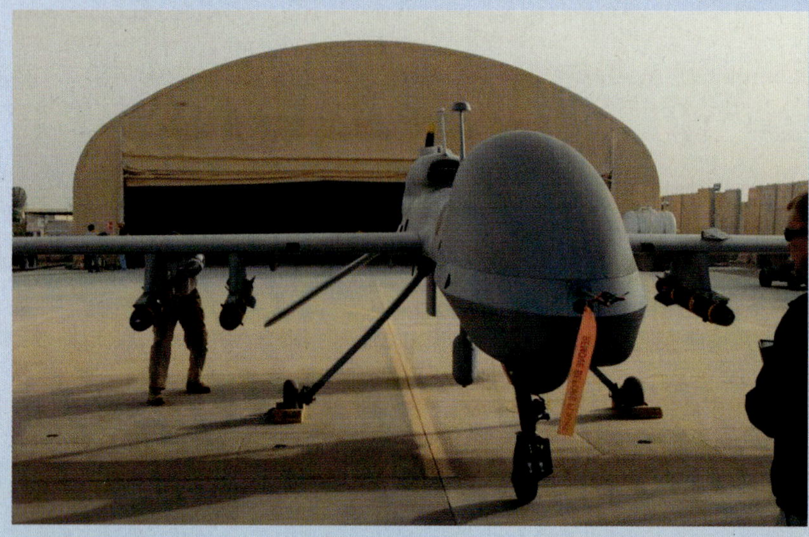

As the wars in Afghanistan and Iraq turned into long drawn-out occupations, the US Army turned its attention to providing its frontline combat units with unmanned aerial vehicles (UAV) to monitor insurgent activity.

The success of the US Air Force's General Atomics MQ-1B Predator and MQ-9A Reaper prompted the US Army to order a derivative of the successful drone in 2005 to replace its RQ-5 Hunter UAVs.

The project was initially called the Sky Warrior and the aim was to acquire 11 units, with each comprising five ground control stations and 12 air vehicles. General Atomics,

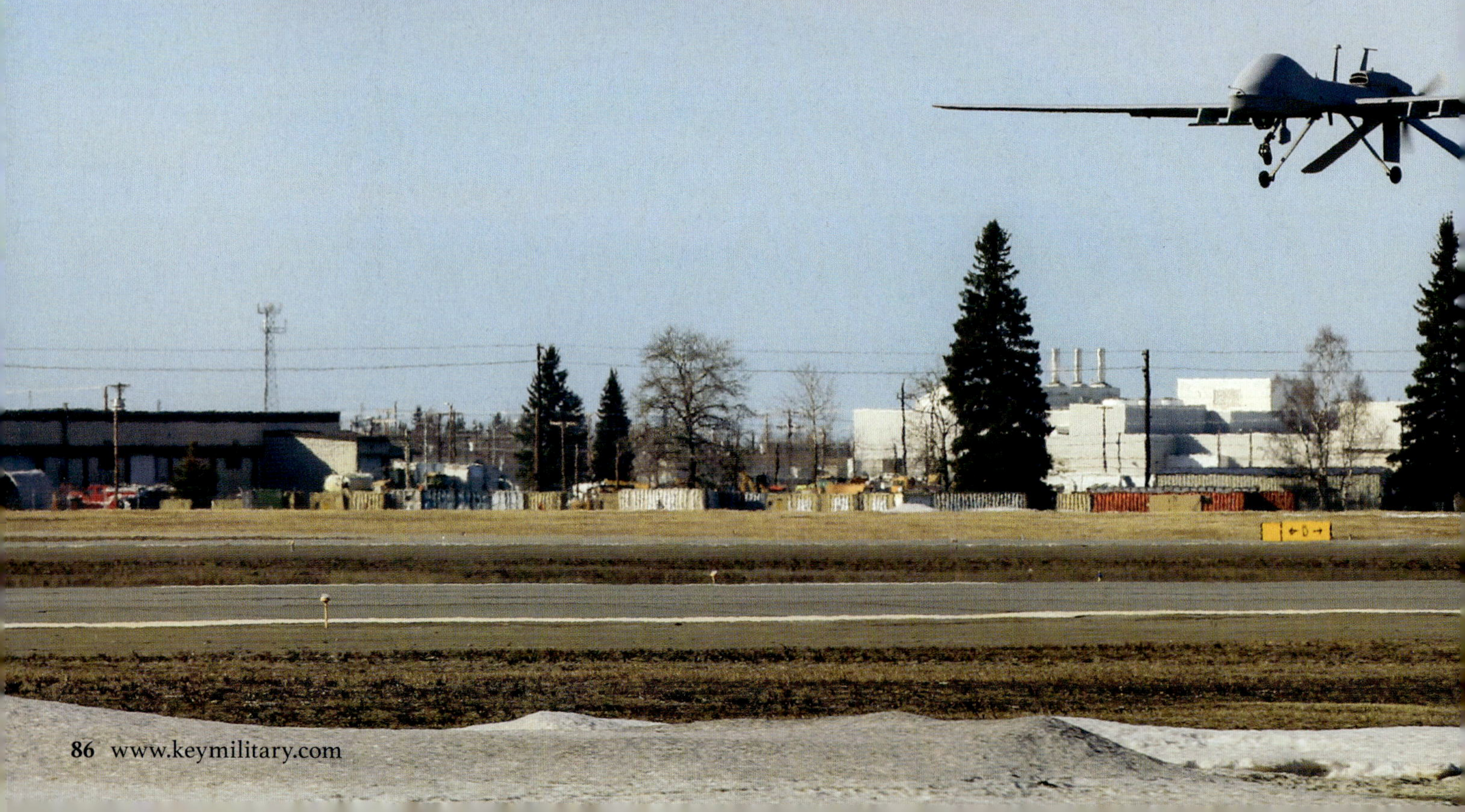

the company that built the USAF Predators, was contracted to adapt the UAV to meet the needs of the US Army. Unlike the US Air Force, which controlled its drones deployed across the globe from command centres in the USA via satellite communications, the US Army was more interested in a UAV that could support its divisions, brigades and battalions in battlefield scenarios.

At first, the project was plagued by technical problems, including software glitches and poor manufacturing quality. The drone was not initially intended to be armed and the retrofitting of this capability in 2010 delayed the fielding of the system. There was a spate of crashes in the early years of service.

In 2010, the project was re-designated the MQ-1C Gray Eagle and it was modified to fit four weapons pylons to its wings to allow up to four AGM-114 Hellfire missiles or other precision-guided weapons to be carried.

The MQ-1C's nose fairing was enlarged to house a synthetic aperture radar/ground moving target indicator (SAR/GMTI) system in addition to an electro-optical camera mounted in a rotating turret under its nose. Operators can fuse infrared imagery and use the SAR to scan and detect changes in terrain such as tyre tracks, footprints and buried improvised explosive devices when performing a second scan.

ABOVE: A MQ-1C Gray Eagle of the 1st Combat Aviation Brigade taxis on a runway during a training exercise at the US Marine Corps Air Ground Combat Center at Twentynine Palms in California. (USMC, LANCE CPL SHANE T BEAUBIEN)

MQ-1C GRAY EAGLE

Power plant:	1 × Thielert Centurion 1.7 heavy-fuel engine
Wingspan:	17m (56ft)
Length:	8.5m (28ft)
Height:	2.1m (6ft 11in)
Max take-off weight:	1,633kg (3,600lb)
Maximum speed:	309kph (192mph)
Armament:	4 × hardpoints, carrying 4 × AGM-114 Hellfire air-to-ground missiles or 8 × AIM-92 Stinger air-to-air missiles or 4 × GBU-44/B Viper Strike guided bombs

BELOW: The MQ-1C Gray Eagle air vehicle evolved from the original USAF MQ-1 Predator, but was extensively modified during its development for the US Army. (US ARMY)

ABOVE: The US Army now routinely uses the MQ-1C Gray Eagle during training exercises and combat operations around the world. (USMC, LANCE CPL SHANE T BEAUBIEN)

It has subsequently been fitted with electronic warfare systems to jam the radio signals used to activate insurgent improvised explosive devices and eavesdrop on enemy communications traffic.

The first Gray Eagles were deployed to Iraq in 2010 as part of an operational test and evaluation mission with the 1st Infantry Division. Four MQ-1Cs of the 160th Special Operations Aviation Regiment (Airborne) – SOAR(A) – first arrived in Afghanistan in December 2010 for a trial deployment in support of US Special Operations Forces (SOF).

Trials were successfully completed in 2012, and full-rate production got under way with the intention of equipping 15 companies with the system. The aim

BELOW: The MQ-1C 25M variant of the Gray Eagle features extended range, better sensors and communications links. (GENERAL ATOMICS)

was to assign one Gray Eagle company to each active-duty combat aviation brigade (CAB), as well as supporting the 160th SOAR(A) and training units. By 2025, 204 MQ-1C air vehicles had been delivered to the US Army to complete the fielding of the system across the active-duty CABs.

It is now routine for MQ-1C companies to deploy alongside CABs to Iraq and Syria as part of Operation Inherent Resolve in ongoing missions to defeat Islamic State insurgents. The drones have also been deployed to Eastern Europe under Operation Atlantic Resolve to deter Russian aggression against NATO allies. Other Gray Eagles have operated in South Korea to patrol the demilitarised zone with communist North Korea.

The 160th SOAR(A) quickly saw the potential of the MQ-1C to support SOF missions. Two full companies, each comprising five ground control stations and 12 air vehicles, were acquired by the regiment from 2010 onwards. The regiment's E Company was sent to Iraq in 2014 to fly daily reconnaissance and strike missions against Islamic State insurgents in Iraq and Syria.

As with US Air Force Special Operations Command MQ-1 and MQ-9 Reaper squadrons, the 160th SOAR(A) created an elite cadre of UAV operators who are specially trained to work with SOF. Unlike their USAF counterparts who operate Reapers from the safety of control centres in the United States, the

MQ-1C companies are often forward deployed into overseas theatres of operation. Their command-and-control centres are co-located in deployed SOF headquarters close to the action.

Gray Eagles from 160th SOAR(A) contingents have taken turns to deploy on counter-terrorist missions in Africa, including operating over Somalia, Mali and Niger. The remains of two MQ-1Cs have been revealed in media reports from Niger since 2020.

A programme of improvements was launched that resulted in the Gray Eagle 25M variant, which incorporates advanced datalinks, upgraded HFE 2.0 engines, open architecture design and ground systems to match electronic threats and sustain expeditionary flights in complex environments.

The new Gray Eagle variant offers more than 40 hours of flight endurance and can operate at altitudes above 29,000ft, as well as supporting an array of new weapons and sensor payloads, including advanced electro-optical sensors, synthetic aperture radar, electronic warfare systems and long-range communications relay equipment.

It boasts a strengthened airframe designed for higher durability and greater payload capacity. It is powered by a new heavy-fuel engine that provides increased power output, improved fuel efficiency and better performance in extreme environments. Additional upgrades include triple-redundant flight control systems, autonomous taxi and take-off/landing capabilities and an advanced datalink suite to enable secure, resilient communications in GPS-denied or electronically contested environments. A redesigned tail structure and enhanced wing design support greater lift and stability, further improving mission endurance and sensor effectiveness.

In December 2023, General Atomics was awarded a $389m contract for an undisclosed number of 25M variants. The new variant boasts an improved Eagle Eye synthetic aperture radar, which can locate targets at up to 201km. This will allow the detection of smaller drones, loitering munitions and airborne weapons in flight.

Twelve Gray Eagle 25Ms were ordered for the Army National Guard in June 2024 to allow the first reserve component combat aviation brigades to operate the MQ-1C family of UAVs. Deliveries of the drones are to begin in 2027. In April 2025, US Defense Secretary Pete Hegseth announced plans to halt the procurement of additional MQ-1Cs, citing vulnerability to enemy air defences. An upgrade programme to improve the drone's sensors so it can stay at a safe distance from targets is under consideration.

ABOVE: US Army National Guard units are receiving an initial batch of a dozen MQ-1C 25M Gray Eagles. (GENERAL ATOMICS)

BELOW: The US Army is looking to the MQ-1C 25M variant as part of drone swarms to overwhelm enemy air defences. (GENERAL ATOMICS)

UH-72 Lakota

Supporting the Home Front

ABOVE: A UH-72A Lakota assigned to the South Carolina Army National Guard flies over the state's major hurricane escape routes during an evacuation exercise with state and local law enforcement agencies. (US ARMY NATIONAL GUARD, STAFF SGT ROBY DI GIOVINE)

At the start of this century, the US Army began hunting for a modern light helicopter to replace hundreds of ageing Bell UH-1H/V Iroquois, Bell TH-67 Creek and Bell OH-58A/C Kiowa helicopters in non-combat support and training roles.

Eurocopter, now Airbus Helicopters, won the Light Utility Helicopter (LUH) competition in June 2006 for the replacement helicopter with a version of the EC-145. This was a well-established product, with more than 1,600 in use with civil and military operators around the world.

The winning helicopter was soon dubbed the UH-72A Lakota in US Army service and an initial production contract for the first 345 helicopters was placed in October 2006. Airbus started building the helicopters at its site in Columbus, Mississippi, from kits shipped from Europe, but switched to full local production in 2009.

In line with US Army tradition to name its helicopters after Native

RIGHT: 121st Medical Company (Air Ambulance), a National Guard unit from Fort Belvoir, Virginia, took its UH-72A Lakota helicopters to provide safety coverage at Hohenfels and Grafenwoehr Training Areas in Germany for a year in 2011. (US ARMY)

Americans, the UH-72 honours the Lakota tribe of the Great Sioux Nation in North and South Dakota. In 2012, Lakota tribal elders blessed two UH-72 helicopters at the Standing Rock Reservation in North Dakota.

The idea was for Army National Guard UH-72s to provide homeland security, disaster response missions and medical evacuations within the continental USA. This was to allow the more expensive UH-60 and other types to be freed up for frontline service overseas. Dedicated security and support units were formed to operate at sites spread across almost every state, so they could rapidly respond to requests from state and other local authorities for military aviation support.

The active-duty US Army Aviation Branch bought the UH-72A to be its basic pilot and air crew training helicopter, to be based primarily at the US Army Aviation Center of Excellence at Fort Rucker in Alabama.

The US Army took delivery of 461 UH-72A models for use by its active-duty and reserve components by 2020, when the Army National Guard started to receive 18 upgraded UH-72Bs – these incorporate improvements that have already been installed on the mainstream civilian version of the helicopter, including a fenestron tail rotor or ducted fan, more powerful engines, enhanced avionics and a fully automated FADEC for better engine control.

The US Army is considering further orders of more B model helicopters to replace older variants and modifications to improve the performance of the A models.

AIRBUS UH-72A LAKOTA	
Powerplant: 2 × Turbomeca Arriel 1E2 turboshaft	
Length: 13.03m (42ft 9in)	
Height: 3.45m (11ft 4in)	
Max take-off weight: 3,585kg (7,904lb)	
Maximum speed: 268kph (167mph)	
Range: 685km (426 miles)	
Crew: 1 or 2 pilots	
Capacity: 9 troops or 2 stretchers and medical crew	

ABOVE: The UH-72A Lakota is based on the Airbus/Eurocopter EC-145 design; more than 1,600 examples have been sold around the world since first flying in 1999. (CURIMEDIA)

LEFT: The South Carolina Army National Guard was the first unit to receive the upgraded UH-72B variant of the Lakota, in February 2023. (US ARMY)

Airlift, Utility and Special Missions

US Army fixed wing aircraft

ABOVE: RC-12 intelligence-gathering aircraft of the 3rd Military Intelligence Battalion are based at Desiderio Army Airfield inside the Camp Humphreys garrison in South Korea. (US ARMY, PATRICK BRAY)

BELOW: Fixed wing aviators undergo training on the C-12U Huron at US Army Flight School at Dothan Airport in Alabama, under an outsourcing contract run by CAE. (US ARMY, 2ND LT HANNAH LAMB)

During World War Two, US Army generals made extensive use of light aircraft to visit their troops and get a grandstand view of the frontline. Today's top brass also needs to be able move round the continental US and operational theatres overseas to keep on top of the latest developments.

For the past 50 years the US Army has made extensive use of the Beechcraft King Air family of twin-turboprop light utility aircraft in transport, special missions and training roles. The majority of 95 C-12 transport aircraft currently in US Army service are assigned to 52 Operational Support Airlift Command (OSACOM) detachments of the Army National Guard and US Army Reserve, which each flying two or three aircraft at locations across the US. In time of conflict, OSACOM detachments have been relocated to overseas operational theatres.

The US Army currently operates around 150 Model 200 and Model 300/350 King Air variants under the current designation of C-12 Huron. The first Model 200 aircraft were initially designated U-25As when they entered service in 1974, before being changed to C-12A for use as liaison and general personnel transport. The aircraft was essentially an off-the-shelf Super King Air 200 powered by Pratt & Whitney Canada PT6A-41 engines.

Beechcraft then produced the enhanced Model 300/350, which boasted a cleaned-up airframe and more powerful PT6A-60A engines, which had redesigned cowlings due to the reshaped engine air intakes. As a result, the aircraft's maximum take-off weight was increased to 6,400kg. The enhanced Super King Air family of aircraft have been in continuous production since 1974, with steady improvements being introduced over time.

The US Army aircraft initially designated the Model 200 and

300/350 variants as C-12 or UC-12. These were purpose-built for the military and were treated by Beechcraft and the Federal Aviation Authority as the separate A200 series. They are used for various duties, including embassy support, medical evacuation and passenger and light cargo transport. Some are modified with surveillance systems for various missions, including the early versions of the RC-12 Guardrail electronic intelligence (ELINT) aircraft. Progressive updates have taken place and several variants of the Model 200 series remain in services. A number of RC-12s based on the Model 200 airframe have been upgraded by the US Army to incorporate Model 350 features, including enhanced PT6A-67 engines and structural modifications. The most recent of these is the RC-12X, with 14 being delivered to the US Army from 2011.

More recently, the US Army has focused on the King Air 350-based variants with the C-12S being used for utility roles, with seating for eight to 15 passengers and a quick cargo conversion capability.

From 2014, the US Army received former USAF MC-12W Liberty surveillance aircraft, which were based on the Model 350 airframe, and it has modified these for other special mission roles. These are known as the MC-12S Enhanced Medium Altitude Reconnaissance and Surveillance System (EMARSS).

The US Army also operates three Beechcraft 1900C variants, which are airliners configured to move small groups of personnel and are designated as C-12J. Other specialist transport aircraft operated by the army include 27 Citation Encores, 11 turboprop Fairchild C-26E Metroliners and one Gulfstream IV/C-20H executive jet.

US Army Special Operations Aviation Command has its own fleets of transport aircraft to move around its personnel and cargo, as well as for conducting parachute training for its soldiers. This currently includes five CASA C-212 Aviocar 5s and seven Alenia C-27J Spartan airlifters.

Training for US Army pilots and aircrew destined to crew fixed wing aircraft is carried out under a commercial contract by CAE at Dothan Airport in Alabama, using 11 C-12Us and six Grob G120TPs provided by the US Army.

Four Beechcraft T-6D Texan II training aircraft have been modified by the US Army for operational support, testing, utility and chase plane roles.

ABOVE: The US Army ordered 60 C-12A Huron utility aircraft and upgraded many of them to C-variant standard with improved engines. (MIKE FREER)

BELOW: C-12U Herons used by E Company, 1st Battalion, 214th Aviation Regiment are the US Army's only fixed-wing unit permanently based in Europe and Africa. The unit is home based at Wiesbaden Army Airfield in Germany. (US ARMY, MASTER SGT RYAN C MATSON)

US ARMY AVIATION

Since the early 1990s, the US Army's Military Intelligence Branch has operated a fleet of fixed wing surveillance aircraft based on de Havilland Canada (DHC) Dash 7 and 8 families. These have been progressively modernised and fitted with a range of electro-optical video cameras, radar and communications intelligence (COMINT) sensor packages.

The DHC-7, popularly known as the Dash 7, is a turboprop-powered regional airliner with short take-off and landing (STOL) performance. It first flew in 1975 and the US Army bought its first examples in the early 1990s to fill gaps left by the retirement of the Grumman OV-1 Mohawk. At its peaks in 2002, the US Army operated seven Dash 7 airframes modified under the Airborne Reconnaissance Low programme, as well as one basic aircraft as an aircrew trainer. These were designated O-5s, with the imagery intelligence platforms termed O-5A ARL-I and the COMINT version known as the EO-5B ARL-C; these capabilities were eventually combined into a single version, dubbed the O-5C ARL-M (for multi-sensor). Until 2004, this version was known as the RC-7B. Only three EO-5Cs remained in service in early 2025.

RIGHT: An RC-12X Guardrail is the latest variant of the aircraft, which features enhanced sensors, communications and flight deck avionics. (US ARMY)

BELOW: The US Army Golden Knights Parachute Team uses the C-147A or Dash-8 to support its participation in more than 100 events every year. (USMC, LANCE CPL ISAAC VELASCO)

The DHC-8 or Dash 8 is a regional airliner powered by two Pratt & Whitney Canada PW150s, which was upgraded from the Dash 7 with improved cruise performance and lower operational costs, but without STOL performance. The US Army bought six of them for conversion into RO-6As Airborne Reconnaissance Low-Enhanced (ARL-E) aircraft. Two of them remained in service in early 2025.

It is intended that that US Army will replace all of its manned fixed wing intelligence gathering aircraft with a new platform based on the Bombardier Global 6500 executive jet under the High Accuracy Detection and Exploitation System (HADES) programme. Two testbeds have been operated for the US Army by industry partners to develop the technology for the HADES aircraft. Bombardier Challenger 600/650 business jets, known as the Airborne Reconnaissance and Targeting Multi-Mission Intelligence System, or ARTEMIS, have been operated in Europe by Leidos. The other demonstrator aircraft – dubbed the Airborne Reconnaissance and Electronic Warfare System (ARES) – has been operating in the Pacific theatre by L3Harris Technologies. It is based on a Global Express 6500 airframe.

In August 2024, the Sierra Nevada Corporation was selected to be the prime HADES contractor to replace the RC-12 family of aircraft and ARL platforms. They were given an initial contract to convert three airframes, which will eventually be part of a fleet of between 6 to 12 aircraft. The US Army said they will have a mix of sensors, including signals intelligence, synthetic aperture radar/moving target indicator and additional unspecified capabilities.

ABOVE: A US Army Reserve C-12V Huron arrives at the US Naval Support Activity Naples in Italy during an intra-theatre transport mission in the European Command area of responsibility. (US NAVY, MASS COMMUNICATION SPECIALIST 2ND CLASS DONAVAN K PATUBO)

BELOW: US Army Special Operations Forces troopers use CASA 212s to carry out parachute jump training. (US ARMY, STAFF SGT SHARILYN WELLS)

Replacing the RQ-7 Shadow

A new tactical UAV for the US Army

ABOVE: The Shadow was teamed with AH-64Es in air cavalry reconnaissance squadrons to hunt down targets on complex battlefields. (USMC)

BELOW: The RQ-7 Shadow gave stalwart service for more than 20 years, but was retired in April 2024 to make way for a new system by 2026. (US ARMY NATIONAL GUARD, CAPT TRAVIS MUELLER)

Up to April 2024, the US Army's main battalion-level unmanned aerial vehicle (UAV), or drone, was the AAI RQ-7 Shadow. It was launched by a catapult and returned to land on a short strip before being brought to a halt by a tail hook that caught on an arrester wire.

This was one of the first US-designed and built drones that took the place of initial systems based on Israeli technology. The Shadow's main sensor was a thermal imaging camera mounted in a turret under the drone's nose. Imagery was them downloaded in real time via a datalink to a ground control station, up to 100km away.

A Shadow system comprised two ground control station (GCS) cabins mounted on the back of a High Mobility Multipurpose Wheeled Vehicle (HMMWV). Each GCS vehicle towed a datalink antenna terminal. A support HMMWV was used to tow the launch catapult and arrester equipment. Video imagery was received and monitored in the GCS cabin, by a team of analysts, who then relayed it to frontline commanders. The air vehicle had an endurance of up to five-and a-half hours.

The US Army had hoped to buy a replacement for the Shadow with the Future Tactical Uncrewed Aircraft System (FTUAS) with drone-makers Griffon and Textron offering rival products in a competition. As a result of US Defense Secretary Pete Hegseth's Army Transformation Initiative announced in May 2025, this competition was halted. Under Hegseth's plans it is still intended to buy a Group 3-class drone to replace the old RQ-7, but the US Army wants industry to come back with new ideas. The new drone would have longer range, strike capabilities, be networked and able to employ jamming technology. This new drone would be able to operate in swarms to overwhelm enemy air defences. It is intended to be in service from 2026.

Mini Drones

Eyes of the Soldier

Each US Army infantry unit is being provided with its own mini drones under the Rucksack Portable Uncrewed Aircraft System (RPUAS) Family project. These systems provide battalions and below ground units with situational awareness and force protection. The systems are in the process of replacing the existing mini-drone systems, including AeroVironment RQ-11 Ravens and RQ-20 Pumas.

SHORT RANGE RECONNAISSANCE (SRR)

The Skydio RQ-28A is the US Army's first quadcopter drone that has been bought as a programme of record, rather than an interim purchase for wartime service. First fielding of the RQ-28A was completed in early November 2024 to the 3rd Battalion, 75th Ranger Regiment at Fort Benning in Georgia. It provides infantry platoons with 30-minute flight endurance, 3km operational range and an electro-optical thermal imaging payload.

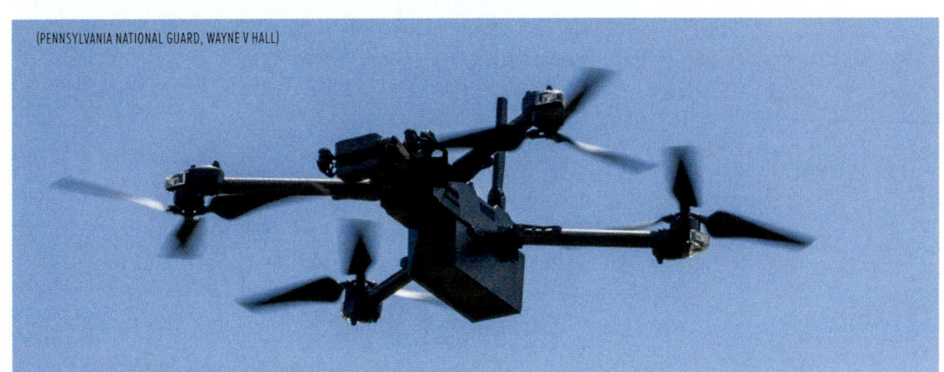
(PENNSYLVANIA NATIONAL GUARD, WAYNE V HALL)

MEDIUM RANGE RECONNAISSANCE (MRR)

The PDW C100 is a vertical take-off and landing drone that provides US Army infantry companies with a medium-range reconnaissance capability. Specific roles include reconnaissance, surveillance, target acquisition, communications relay and kinetic and non-kinetic payload delivery. The system weighs just 21lb and is small enough to fit in a soldier's rucksack. It has a range of up to 5km.

(PERFORMANCE DRONE WORKS)

LONG RANGE RECONNAISSANCE (LRR)

The final element of the RPUAS project is a long-range drone, but this has not yet been selected. A strong contender is the AeroVironment P550, a highly modular battery-powered unmanned aerial system that can take off and land vertically and is able to carry up to 15lb of munitions and sensors. It has a range of between 40 and 60km.

(US ARMY, CAPT THOMAS MCCARTY)

Fire for Effect

Missiles and guns

HELLFIRE

Lockheed Martin's Missiles & Fire Control division produces the AGM-114 Hellfire guided missile, which is the US Army Aviation Branch's main aerial weapon. It is integrated with the Boeing AH-64E Apache, Sikorsky UH-60, Boeing MH-6 Little Bird and General Atomics MC-1C Gray Eagle. It was developed specifically for use on the original McDonnell Douglas AH-64A Apache and went into production in 1982. Early variants only had semi-active laser guidance. Targets could be designated by the Apache's gunner, as well as forward an air controller on the ground or in other aircraft. The weapon has proved to be highly effective and very accurate, with a circular error probable (CEP) of less than a metre.

It was originally developed under the name Heliborne laser, fire-and-forget missile, which led to the nickname name 'Hellfire' coming into widespread use. The US Army originally wanted the Apache to strike at Soviet armoured divisions, so the first Hellfire missiles had high explosive anti-tank or shaped charges to penetrate armour. The follow-on AH-64D Longbow

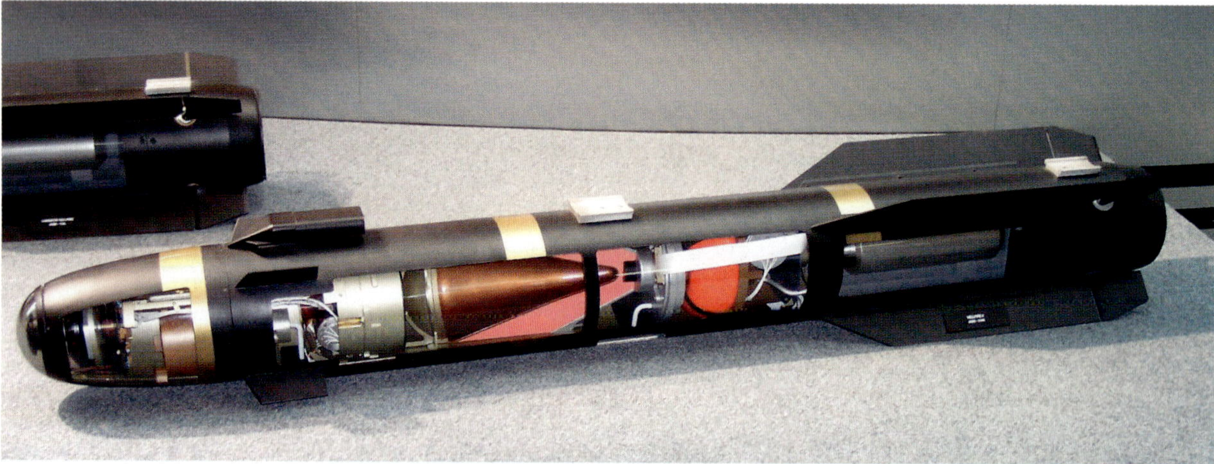

RIGHT: The AGM-114M Hellfire II had extended range over earlier variants of the missile. (STAHLKOCHER)

BELOW: The AGM-179 joint air-to-ground missile is being developed to replace the long serving AGM-114 Hellfire as the main stand-off weapon employed on the AH-64 Apache. Here, an AGM-179 is being live fired on the Cibola Range at Yuma Test Center, Arizona. (US ARMY)

The AGM-114 Hellfire is the primary stand-off weapon of the US Army's MQ-1C Gray Eagle family of UAVs. (USAF)

Four AGM-114 Hellfires can be carried on each AH-64 weapon pylon. If the tactical situation demands it, up to four pylons of missiles can be carried. (DOD PHOTO, SGT ALFREDO BARRAZA JR)

Apache variant was fitted with the Longbow millimetre radar, which could locate enemy tanks at night or in bad weather. This helicopter was provided with a version of the Hellfire with a guidance unit that could receive targeting data from the Longbow radar.

When the US Army mounted the Global War on Terrorism across Afghanistan, Iraq and into North Africa, the insurgent groups did not have many tanks or other heavy equipment. Commanders requested versions of the Hellfire to be developed to enable their helicopter crews to engage pick-up trucks, buildings or bunkers. This resulted in a suite of warheads including blast/fragmentation, incendiary and metal augmented charge (thermobaric).

Once General Atomics MQ-1 Predator, MQ-9 Reaper and the MQ-1C Gray Eagle UAVs started to be armed from 2001, they needed dedicated versions of Hellfire to make it more suitable for precision strikes on high-value targets, such as insurgent leaders. The AGM-114P and AGM-114R featured smaller warheads to reduce collateral damage. A highly classified version, the AGM-114R9X, which has no explosive warhead and six blades, is designed to rip open soft-skinned vehicles and kill their occupants. It has reportedly been used in action in Iraq and Syria since 2017.

The US Army is aiming to replace the Hellfire with the Lockheed Martin AGM-179 joint air-to-ground missile (JAGM), which has a range of up to 16 kilometres to allow Apaches to stay out of range of enemy anti-aircraft missiles. As an interim solution, in 2020 the US Army started fielding the Israeli-made Rafael Spike NLOS missile for its AH-64Es. ➤

HELLFIRE VARIANTS

AGM-114A
Produced: 1982-1992
Range: 8,700yd (8,000m)
Guidance: Semi-active laser homing (SALH)
Warhead: 18lb (8kg) shaped charge HEAT

AGM-114B/C
Produced: 1982-1992
Range: 8,700yd (8,000m)
Guidance: Semi-active laser homing (SALH)
Warhead: 18lb (8kg) shaped charge HEAT.

AGM-114F/FA Interim Hellfire
Produced: 1991-1994
Range: 8,700yd (8,000m)
Guidance: Semi-active laser homing (SALH)
Warhead: 18lb (8kg) shaped charge HEAT. Tandem-charge.

AGM-114K/K2/K2A Hellfire II
Produced: 1993-2018
Range: 12,000yd (11,000m)
Guidance: Semi-active laser homing (SALH) with electro-optical countermeasures hardening.
Warhead: 20lb (9kg) tandem shaped charge HEAT

AGM-114L Hellfire Longbow
Produced: 1995-2005, 2016 to date
Range: 8,700yd (8,000m)
Guidance: Fire and forget millimetre-wave (MMW) radar seeker coupled with inertial guidance
Warhead: 20lb (9kg) tandem shaped charge high-explosive anti-tank HEAT

AGM-114M Hellfire II (Blast Frag)
Produced: 1998-2010
Range: 12,000yd (11,000m)
Guidance: Semi-active laser homing (SALH)
Warhead: Blast fragmentation/incendiary
Weight: 108lb (49kg)
Length: 71in (180cm)

AGM-114N Hellfire (MAC)
Produced: 2003-2018
Range: 12,000yd (11,000m)
Guidance: Semi-active laser homing/millimetre-wave radar seeker
Warhead: Metal augmented charge (thermobaric)

AGM-114P/P+ Hellfire II (For UAV)
Produced: 2003-2012
Range: 12,000yd (11,000m)
Guidance: Semi-active laser homing (SALH)
Warhead: Shaped charge or blast fragmentation

AGM-114R Hellfire II (Hellfire Romeo)
Produced: 2012 to date
Range: 8,700yd (8,000m)
Guidance: Semi-active laser homing (SALH)
Warhead: Multi-function warhead, reduced explosive weight for low collateral damage

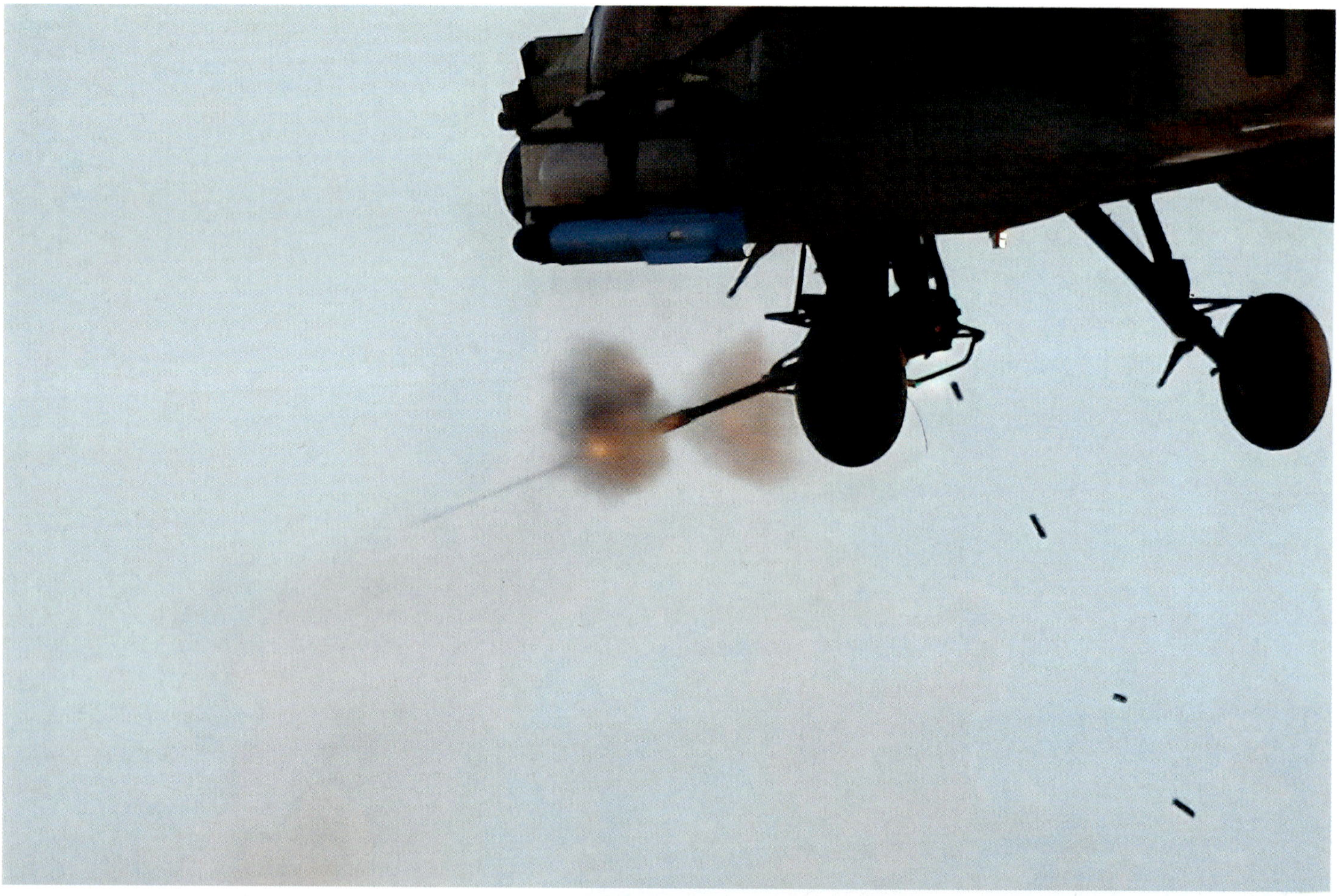

ABOVE: An M230 chain gun is mounted just under the AH-64's nose and can be slaved onto targets by the gunner's IHADSS helmet sight. (NEHEMIA GERSHUNI-AYLHO)

M230

The M230 chain gun is the main area weapon system for the Boeing AH-64D/E Apache attack helicopter. It is mounted on the chin turret, powered by an electric motor and can fire 30mm linkless ammunition at a rate of 625 rounds per minute. The air-cooled gun's practical rate of fire is about 300 rounds per minute with a 10-minute cooling period. Spent casings are ejected downwards below the helicopter.

The mount on the AH-64 uses secondary hydraulics to move the gun, which are 'slaved' to the helicopter gunner's integrated helmet and display sighting system (IHADSS). This allows the gunner to look at a target using the helicopter's target acquisition and designation sights, pilot night vision system (TADS/PNVS), instantly bringing the 30mm gun to bear just by pressing its trigger.

AH-64Ds can carry up to 1,200 rounds for the gun, but the newer AH-64Es only carries around 300 rounds because the magazine has been reduced to make room for an additional fuel tank.

The Sikorsky MH-60L Direct Action Penetrator variant of the Black Hawk used by the US Special Operations Forces can also carry the M230 on its external weapon pylons.

RIGHT: The 30mm rounds are loaded into an AH-64D Apache of the 82nd Airborne Division at Forward Operating Base Salerno in the Khowst province of Afghanistan in 2007. (US ARMY, STAFF SGT ISAAC A GRAHAM)

RIGHT: The IHADSS helmet sight allows AH-64 gunners to slew the helicopters cannon on to targets by moving their head. Hellfire and Hydra 70 rockets can also be targeted using the sight. (MOD CROWN COPYRIGHT)

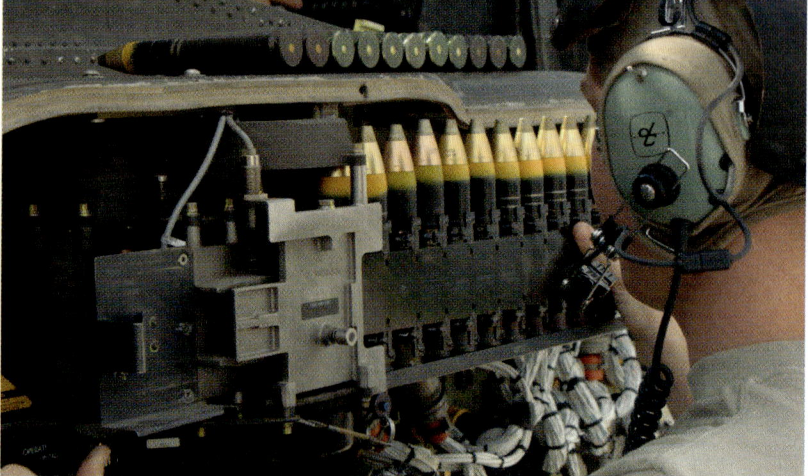

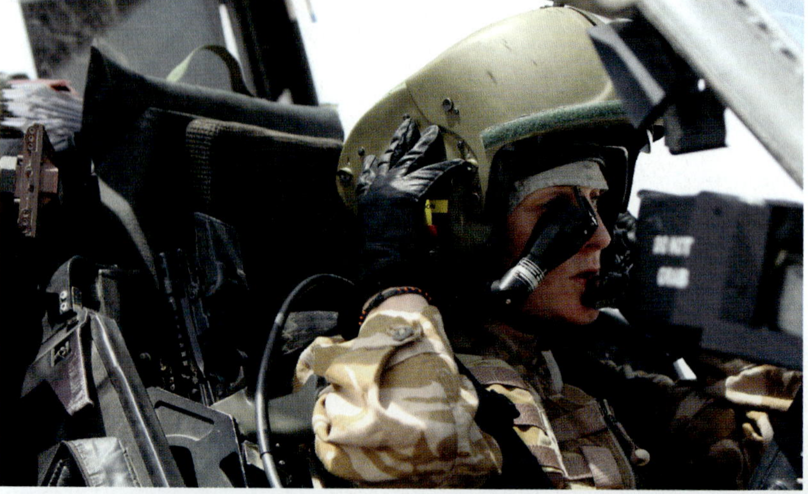

HYDRA 70

To protect friendly troops during close air support missions, US Army helicopters are armed with the Hydra 70 rocket system. This is a 70mm fin-stabilised unguided rocket that is fired from pods that can be loaded with up to 19 rockets.

The Hydra 70 system can be equipped with a variety of warheads and, in more recent versions, a guidance system for point attack. The AGR-20 advanced precision kill weapon system (APKWS) that equips Hydra 70 rockets with a laser guidance kit turns them into precision-guided munitions. The APKWS is approximately one-third the cost and one-third the weight of larger laser-guided bombs or missiles. It has a lower yield that's more suitable for avoiding collateral damage, as well as taking a quarter of the time for ordnance personnel to load and unload. The weapon bridges the gap between the Hydra 70 and AGM-114 Hellfire and provides a cost-effective method of engaging lightly armoured point targets. It has an effective range of up to 11 kilometres.

A suite of around 20 warheads for the Hydra family of rockets is available, including high explosive/ blast fragmentation, smoke, sub-munition dispensing, anti-armour, incendiary, illuminating, smoke, flechette, anti-personnel, red/white phosphorus and penetrators.

The most common warhead for the Hydra 70 rocket is the M151 '10-Pounder', which has a blast radius of 10 metres and a lethal fragmentation radius of 50 metres. The M247 high-explosive anti-tank / high-explosive dual purpose (HEDP) warheads can penetrate 300mm of rolled homogenous armour.

ABOVE: An MH-60M DAP fires a 2.75in Hydra rocket on a test range, demonstrating the weapon's deadly effect. (US ARMY)

BELOW: Hydra-70 rockets can be employed by US Army AH-64, AH-6/MH-6 and UH-60 helicopters. (USMC, SSGT ARTUR SHVARTSBERG)

ABOVE: Teams at forward arming and refuelling points (FARPs) are trained to rapidly reload AH-64s so they can return to the fight. (US ARMY, KEVIN STERLING PAYNE)

Air Assault into the 21st Century

Future long-range assault aircraft

Putting boots in the ground deep inside enemy territory to seize key objectives by surprise has long been a key mission of US Army aviation. Advances in air defence and aircraft technology has led the US Army to look to bring its helicopter fleet up to date to meet the new challenges of the 21st Century.

These ambitions were wrapped up in a programme dubbed Future Vertical Lift (FVL), which incorporated new technology, advanced materials and the development of next-generation networking systems. It took inspiration from the USAF and US Marine Corps Bell-Boeing V-22 Osprey tiltrotor project, which replaced the old Sikorsky MH-53 Pave Lowe and Boeing Vertol CH-46 Sea Stallion helicopters with a machine that could fly twice the range at twice the speed. The Osprey's engines tilted up and down, so it could take off and land like a helicopter, but fly in level flight like a fixed wing aircraft.

The US Army's budgetary and financial turbulence in recent years led to scrapping of the Future Attack Reconnaissance

RIGHT: Air assault operations to land troops far behind enemy lines remains a core capability for the US Army. (US DOD)

BELL MV-25 VALOR

Powerplant:	2 × Rolls-Royce AE 1107F turboshaft engines
Length:	15.4m (50ft 6in)
Width:	24.93m (81ft 8in)
Height:	7m (23ft)
Max take-off weight:	14,000kg (30,865lb)
Cruise speed:	520kph (320mph)
Combat range:	930-1,480km (580-920miles)
Crew:	4
Capacity:	14 troops

BELOW: A Bell V-280 Valor demonstrating high-speed cruise configuration at the 2019 Alliance Air Show at Fort Worth in Texas. (DANAZAR)

ABOVE: The V-280 Valor will be known as the MV-25 when it enters US Army service. (BELL TEXTRON INC)

Aircraft (FARA) project in February 2024, which was meant to take the place Bell OH-58 Kiowa Warrior scout helicopter. The OH-58 was retired in 2014 and its roles taken over by Boeing AH-6E Apache and AAI RQ-7 Shadow UAVs. Aerial reconnaissance is increasingly dominated by drones to reduce the risk to human helicopter crews, so the US Army decided it was not essential to move forward with FARA and, in early 2024, announced its rejigged plans. This entailed buying more drones and confirming the Future Long-Range Assault Aircraft (FLRAA) programme as its primary new equipment project. The idea was to dramatically extend the reach of its air assault and combat casualty evacuation platforms.

The FLRAA is based on the Bell V-280 Valor medium-lift, tiltrotor aircraft. It was selected in 2022 to augment or replace a large number of the Sikorsky UH-60 Black Hawks to provide combat aviation brigades with a long-range, high-speed utility capability with survivability in contested environments. In 2024, the US Army accelerated its plans and committed to getting the V-280 into service by 2030. The new tiltrotor was designated the MV-25 in November 2024.

With enhanced speed and improved range, the Army wants FLRAA to take the mission twice as far, twice as fast, expanding the size of the battlefield and extending the reach of missions.

In a December 2024 briefing on the project, Major General Clair Gill, commander of the US Army Aviation Center of Excellence at Fort Novosel, Alabama, said: "We're watching the very nature of warfare change. The speed of technology is absolutely meteoric." Major General Brett Sylvia, commander of the 101st Airborne Division (Air Assault) at Fort Campbell, Kentucky, added that such swift change is needed because "we can't actually do the large-scale, long-range air assault today with the speed and distance required in modern warfare. What we can do is build the new techniques and procedures, build the doctrine, build the structures, understand the sustainment in order to be able to do that with a faster, future aircraft." He said that such a mission is defined as the ability to deliver one brigade combat team more than 500 miles in a single period of darkness, arriving behind enemy lines able to conduct sustained combat operations.

A recent exercise involved the 101st Division moving a brigade combat team from Fort Campbell to Fort Johnson in Louisiana – a distance of 575 miles. Making the move required establishing two mission support sites, six forward arming and refuelling points and positioning about 1,000 soldiers at those sites in advance for support and security. Sylvia admitted: "It also took us three periods of darkness." However, he said simulations show that by using the FLRAA for such missions instead of the UH-60, the division could take the brigade combat team 575 miles

BELOW: Bell beat the design teams from Sikorsky and Boeing in December 2022 to move forward with the V-280 for the FLRAA. (BELL TEXTRON INC)

in only one period of darkness. This would also cut in half the sustainment and security needed.

Brigadier General Clinton Murray, commander of the US Army Medical Center of Excellence at Joint Base San Antonio, Texas, said the planned long-range rotor aircraft was making a huge difference for transporting and protecting casualties: "The FLRAA will allow casualties to be moved rapidly off the battlefield, giving commanders freedom of movement. The new aircraft will move critically injured soldiers faster, over longer distances, with less need to refuel."

Brigadier General Cain Baker, director for the Future Vertical Lift Cross Functional Team at Redstone Arsenal in Huntsville, Alabama, said that FLRAA will positively impact survivability of warfighters through its extended range, ease of picking up and transferring patients and the fact that

ABOVE: The Bell V-280 Valor incoporates many of the technologies utilised in the V-22 Osprey, but has developed it further and, crucially, made it significantly cheaper to manufacture and operate.
(BELL TEXTRON INC)

RIGHT: Bell's V-280 Valor prototype made an appearance at the 2019 Alliance Air Show at Fort Worth in Texas in 2019.
(DANAZAR)

the aircraft can communicate with the field hospital staff, allowing medical professionals to know what's coming before the aircraft lands. Baker also noted that V-280 maintenance crews at the launch point will understand the health of the aircraft before it returns from a mission.

Brigadier General David Phillips, program executive officer for aviation at Redstone Arsenal, Alabama, said the FLRAA programme shows how the US Army is now engaging in modern aircraft acquisition by going a little slower upfront, with the plan to move faster later: "That means we've got model-based systems engineering. We've got standards and interfaces that are defined down to the individual component level. This will enable US Army aviation to bring new capabilities forward more quickly, making updates and changes timelier."

"The ways of doing acquisition today are markedly different than what was seen in the past, and FLRAA is a great example of that. If you go back and look at the historical timelines for aviation acquisition, this is absolutely an accelerated approach, but it does not sacrifice the rigour in the major programme acquisition." Phillips said Special Operations Command and allies have come on board early with FLRAA project agreements. The allies want to align their resources for when the US starts exporting this machine in the 2030s:

"This is a very transformational branch right now," said Clair Gill. "The FLRAA is one of the US Army's signature modernisation systems representing that change."

The V-280 project took a major step forward in August 2024 when it entered its next development phase after the US Army announced the approval of the FLRAA Milestone B Acquisition Decision Memorandum. The decision came after the successful FLRAA preliminary design review to confirm the V-280 as fit to move into the building of the aircraft. This will see work start on detailed aircraft design and construction of six prototype YMV-25Vs. The final production MV-25 will involve modifications to the prototype V-280's internal layout and mechanical systems.

The US Army has accelerated development of the MV-25, with first fielding now expected in 2028 to the 101st Airborne Division (Air Assault) after the FLRAA's maiden flight in 2026. Initial production is now expected to take place simultaneously to speed up the delivery of initial batches of MV-25s.

ABOVE: The US Army and Bell are working to transition the V-280 demonstrator into a production standard machine in time to enter frontline service after 2030. (BELL TEXTRON INC)

TOP: The US Army hopes to replace almost all of its UH-60 Black Hawks with the MV-25 in the air assault role. (BELL TEXTRON INC)

A New Type of Warfare

Lessons learned from the conflict in Ukraine

ABOVE: Ka-52 co-axial rotor attack helicopters have seen extensive action during the war in Ukraine. (RUSSIAN MINISTRY OF DEFENCE)

The formation of ten Mil Mi-8 helicopters touched down almost simultaneously in the middle of the main runway of Antonov International Airport in the Kyiv suburb of Hostomel. Within minutes, hundreds of Russian paratroopers were in position on the ground, protecting the helicopters as they lifted off.

The coup d'main operation by Russian airborne forces (VDV) to capture an airfield on the outskirts of the Ukrainian capital on February 22, 2022, had begun in a dramatic fashion. Minutes later, a US television crew arrived and started to film the Russian troops fanning out to secure the airfield. So far, so good for the largest and most ambitious air assault operation in Russian or Soviet military history. Within hours, fierce Ukrainian resistance would derail the operation to seize their capital.

RIGHT: Troops of Russia's elite 45th Spetsnaz Brigade were landed in the first wave of Russian helicopters to reach Antonov International Airport. (RUSSIAN MINISTRY OF DEFENCE)

shore, Ukrainian soldiers readied a salvo of Igla heat-seeking man portable surface-to-air missiles (manpads) and started to take aim at the Russian helicopters. As the Mi-8s were landing and Russian paratroopers were on the runway of the airport, the activity was being recorded on camera phones of local people and was soon being posted online.

Ultimately, the Russian airborne assault on Kyiv failed in its strategic aim of toppling the Ukrainian government in a blitzkrieg strike. While the first wave of VDV units had achieved tactical surprise and captured Antonov International Airport, the rapid response of the Ukrainians to block the roads and blow up bridges into Kyiv meant the Russian strike force could not advance much further. Ukrainian resistance along the Russian supply line to Belarus also slowed the build-up of the 35th Army's tanks and heavy artillery. The Russian had lost the battle. Russian President Vladimir Putin was reportedly far from happy at this defeat and news emerged that General Serdyukov had been sacked as commander of the VDV.

Since 2022, the war in Ukraine has thrown up many lessons for army aviators around the world and the US Army has been closely watching what has been happening. The failed air assault was clearly an important moment in the war but, since then, helicopters have been used by both sides in a variety of missions, with varying degrees of success.

The first sign that the mission was underway was earlier in the morning, when a long line of helicopters could be seen flying down the Dnieper River towards Kyiv. As they neared the city, the escorting Kamov Ka-52s, Mil Mi-35 gunships and Mi-8 assault helicopters turned west. On the

In the later months of 2022, the Ukrainian war settled into grinding trench warfare as both sides dug in along more than 1,000 kilometres of frontline. Behind those trench lines, both sides have built up thick air defence networks with thousands of anti-aircraft guns and manpads, backed up by radar-guided surface-to-air missiles (SAMs). This has made it very difficult for either side to safely operate helicopters close to the frontline and almost impossible to penetrate into enemy airspace without running the risk of taking heavy losses. These air defence networks are just too thick to ❯

LEFT: Images from a Russian Ka-52 pilot's Go-pro camera during the air assault on Antonov International Airport. (RUSSIAN MINISTRY OF DEFENCE)

BELOW: More than a 100 Russian combat helicopters were massed in Belarus to support the VDV assault to capture Kiev. (MAXAR TECHNOLOGIES)

RIGHT: Several Russian helicopters were destroyed in a daring Ukrainian drone strike on Kherson airfield in March 2022. (via BELLINGCAT)

BELOW: The Russian Aerospace Force has dispersed its attack helicopters to several forward operating bases to make it harder for the Ukrainians to knock out large numbers in a single strike. (@BRADYAFR)

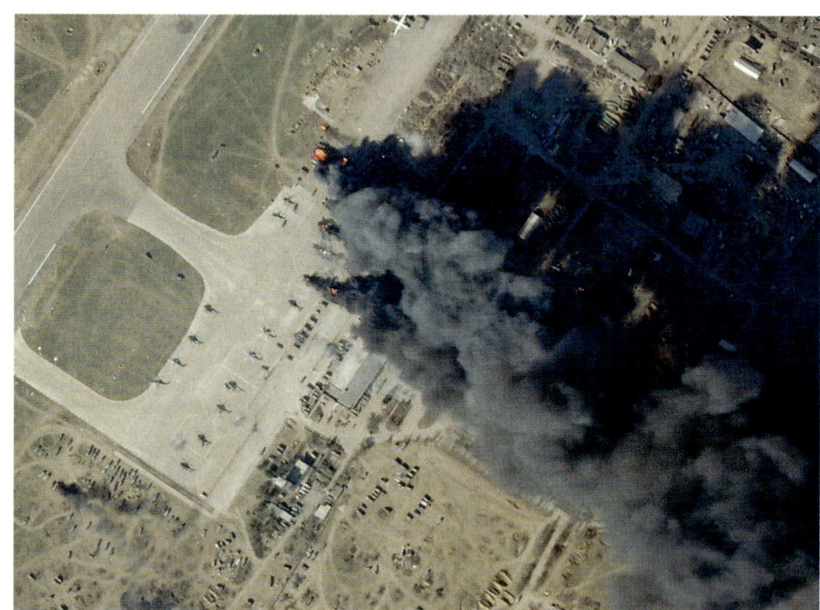

make it possible for helicopter pilots to find a safe route around threats.

To bring rotorcraft firepower to bear on the frontline, Russian and Ukrainian attack helicopters have been forced to operate at ultra-low level and carry out lofting attacks with unguided rockets or guided missiles, so as not to expose themselves to enemy air defence threats by popping up from behind the shelter of terrain. In an attempt to force enemy attack helicopters back from the frontline, both sides started to attack enemy airfields and forward operations bases (FOBs) with long-range rockets, missiles or armed UAVs. Dozens of Russian helicopters have been knocked out by such attacks, forcing them to disperse their rotorcraft into smaller

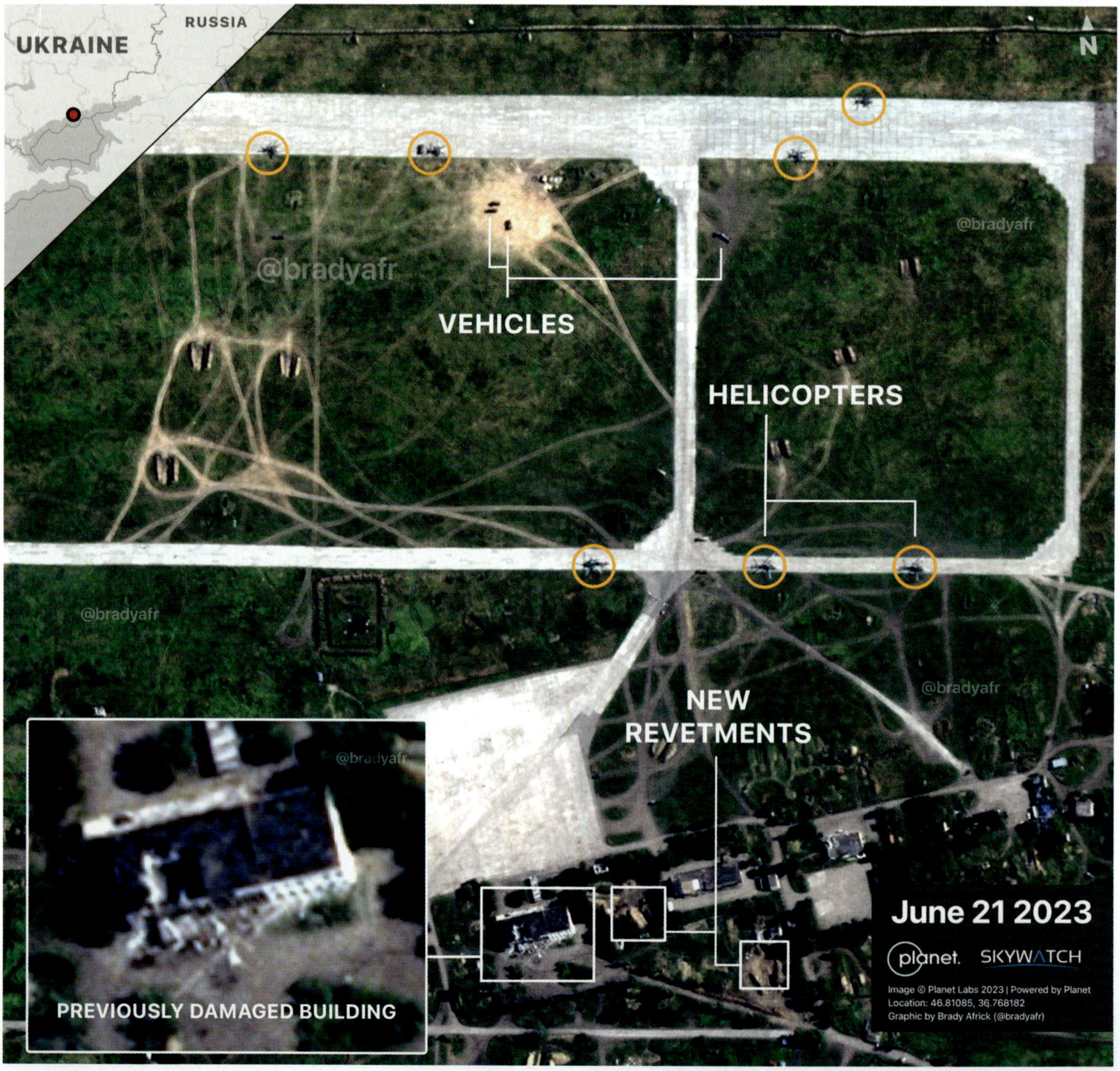

FOBs to complicate Ukrainian targeting.

The Ukrainians have also taken to dispersing their helicopters and aircraft away from their main airfields to field locations. To counter this, the Russians used one-way attack or kamikaze drones to find and destroy Ukrainian helicopters as they move close to frontline.

Perhaps the most significant intervention by attack helicopters came in the summer of 2023, during the ill-fated Ukrainian armoured counter-offensive. This saw columns of western-supplied tanks and armoured vehicles attempting to break through the Russian lines and push south into the strategic Crimean peninsula. A network of minefields, obstacles and trenches was built by the Russians, so when then first wave of Ukrainian tanks pushed forward they quickly got bogged down. At this point, the Russian Ka-52s and Mil Mi-28 attack helicopters were called in to engage the stalled Ukraine columns. From the safety of Russian-controlled territory, the helicopters started to pick off dozens of Ukrainian tanks and vehicles with laser-guided anti-tank missiles. Within weeks, the Ukraine offensive had been halted and hundreds of their armoured vehicles knocked out.

For US Army aviators, the Ukraine war has thrown into stark relief many of their tactics, equipment and operational procedures. The hottest topic is the survivability of helicopters on the modern battlefield. Concerns about this clearly played a part in the decision in February 2004 to cancel the Future Army Reconnaissance Aircraft project in favour of more emphasis on drones to penetrate behind enemy lines to search for targets.

Nevertheless, the US Army continues to believe that air assault operations are still a valid act of war, as long as they are conducted in the right way. It is investing significant resources in the Future Long-Range Assault Aircraft programme, to enable the US Army to deliver troops far behind enemy lines. By extending the range of this new aircraft, the US Army hopes to increase its tactical flexibility and approach options. Air assault operations have long depended on surprise to achieve success, so fielding an air assault aircraft that can fly longer and faster will, in theory, keep their enemies guessing.

A big take-away from the Ukraine war is the need to disperse helicopters and their support vehicles, including fuel tankers, repair trucks and ammunition dumps, to reduce their vulnerability

to attack. The days of massing dozens of helicopters and support vehicles at large FOBs are clearly over. The US Army is looking at ways to operate its helicopters in small-sized groups spread around multiple FOBs that can be easily camouflaged. This requires investment in fuel tankers, ammunition-carrying trucks, airstrips and communications equipment. More engineering support is needed to build a greater number of smaller FOBs and to put in place the necessary security measures, such as metal landing pads and earth berms, to protect helicopters from cluster munitions, as well as the instillation of fuel bladders.

Networked communication and mission planning systems are crucial elements in this new way of warfare,

allowing commanders to plan with their helicopter crews without them having to be in the same location. Only in the final minutes of a major operation will attack and transport helicopters mass to launch their assault.

The proliferation of highly effective air defence systems is forcing the US Army to look at extending the range of its main anti-armour missiles. The AGM-114 Hellfire has given more than 40 years of stalwart service, but it is being outranged by modern air defence systems. Work began on the AGM-179 joint air-to-ground missile (JAGM) several years ago and when it finally enters service later this decade it will double the stand-off attack range of the AH-64E. As a stopgap, the US Army has begun to field the Israeli-made Rafael Spike NLOS on its AH-64Es.

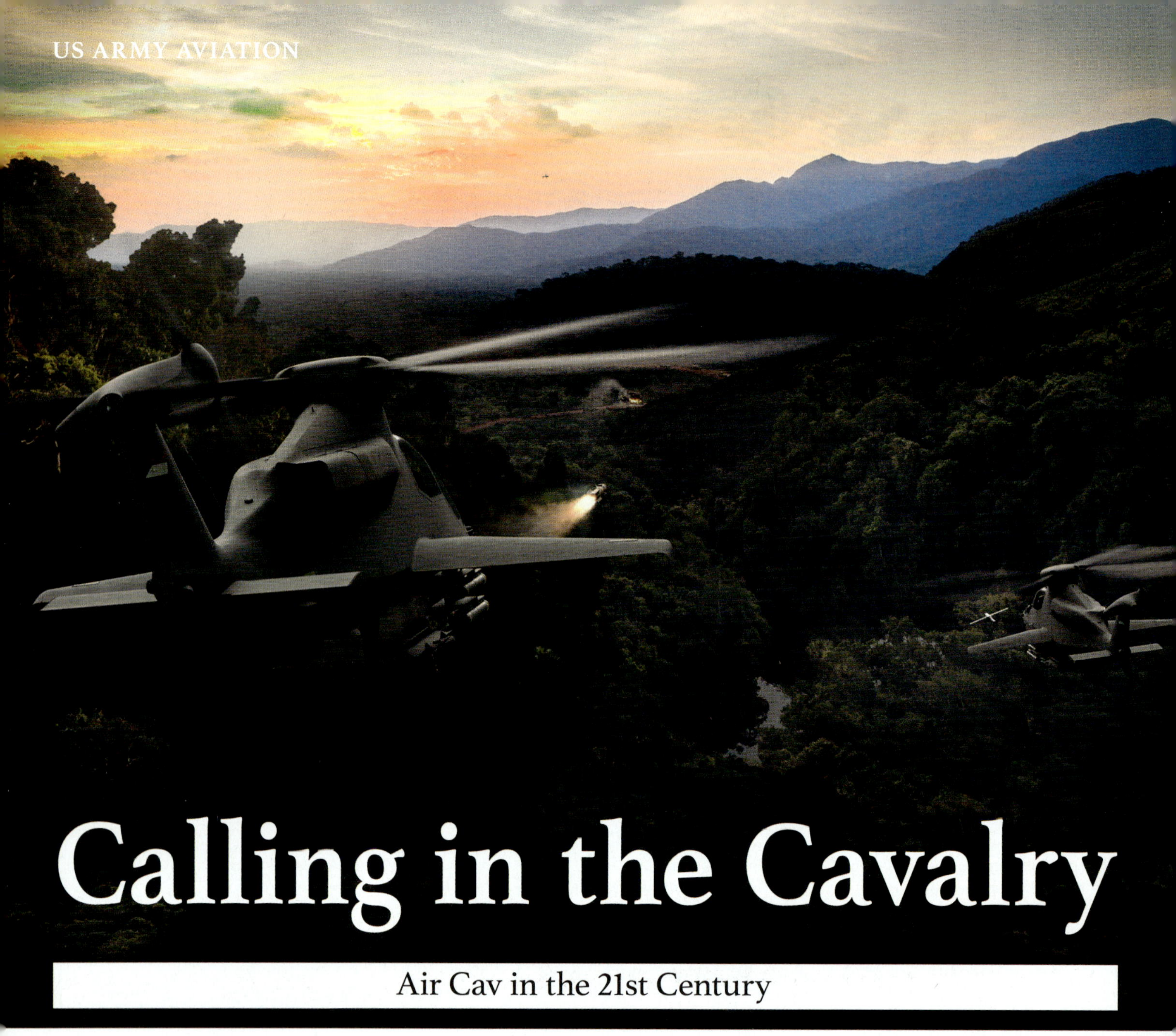

Calling in the Cavalry

Air Cav in the 21st Century

ABOVE: The US Army is building a new generation of tiltrotors to replace its existing fleet of UH-60 Black Hawk air assault helicopters. (BELL TEXTRON)

RIGHT: US Defense Secretary Pete Hegseth and Vice President JD Vance visiting US troops on America's southern border to interdict migrants trying to cross from Mexico. (PETE HEGSETH, VIA X)

Sixty years on from the commitment of the 1st Cavalry Division (Airmobile) to the conflict in Vietnam and the start of the revolution in helicopter warfare, US Army Aviation is on the brink of another watershed.

A return to great power competition and so-called 'peer-on-peer' conflict is bringing to an end the focus of the US Army on the Global War on Terrorism. This is prompting the US Army Aviation Branch to launch a major re-equipment effort and take a new look at its tactics and operational procedures for what the Pentagon calls 'large-scale combat operations'. The return of US President Donald Trump to the White House is also shaking up US defence policy, with a pivot to Asia to challenge China's military power. US Defense Secretary Pete Hegseth is already looking at downsizing the US Army and divesting the Pentagon of military capabilities not relevant to the new era. The so-called 'forever wars' in the Middle East and Africa are set to end as the Pentagon concentrates resources in the Pacific.

The past 25 years have been good for the US Army Aviation Branch. Helicopters and surveillance drones were essential capabilities in the counter-insurgence campaigns of the Global War on Terrorism. US Army combat aviation brigades have had almost all of their helicopters and

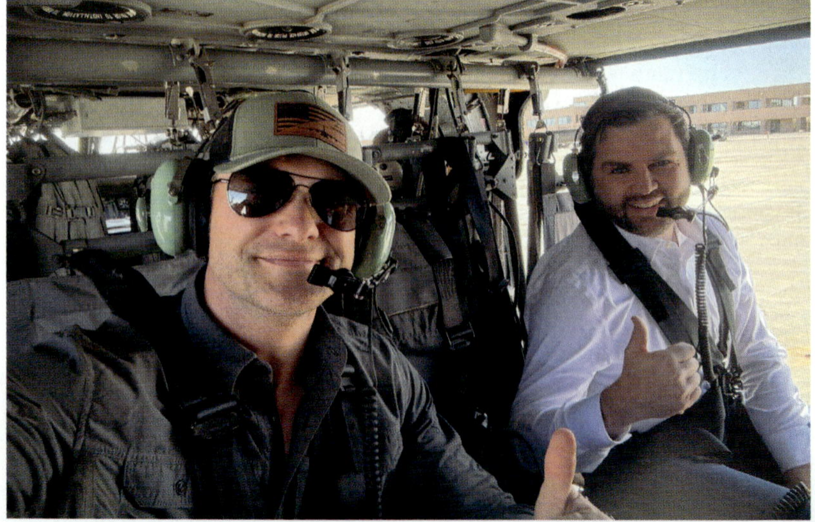

drones replaced or upgraded to enable them to be continuously deployed to fight in Afghanistan, Iraq, Syria and elsewhere. Modernised Boeing AH-64E Apaches, Boeing CH-47F Chinooks, Sikorsky UH-60 M/Vs and Airbus UH-72A/B Lakotas have been fielded to recapitalise the US Army's rotorcraft fleet. The arrival of the General MQ-1C Gray Eagle and an array of small drones also brought the US Army well and truly into the era of UAVs. These are some of the most modern and capable aerial weapons in the world.

Over the past decade, active duty and reserve combat aviation brigades have been deployed on continuous rotations to Afghanistan, Iraq/Syria and Eastern Europe. These missions have ensured that US Army aviators have an unprecedented level of combat experience, which means they are fit to take on all comers.

While the US Army might well be at the top of its game for counter-insurgency operations, it is now clear that the game is about to change. This will require a major reset of the US Army Aviation Branch. The ongoing war in Ukraine has thrown up important lessons about how helicopters and drones can operate and survive in high-intensity warfare against opponents armed with modern air defence weapons. This experience has seen US Army

Aviation revisiting the tactics it developed in the 1980s to counter massed Soviet tank divisions in central Europe. US Army combat aviation brigades that have deployed to Eastern Europe over the past decade have re-learned how to fight as part of combined arms formations, against enemy forces equipped with tanks, artillery and large numbers of armoured vehicles.

A key lesson for the US Army Aviation Branch has been how to survive on increasingly lethal battlefields, where the enemy has the ability to carry out long-range surveillance and rocket strikes against helicopter forward operating bases (FOBs). The US Army is learning to operate in an environment where it is no longer invulnerable and has to be prepared to experience significant ➤

BOTTOM: The current generation of US Army UH-60 Black Hawk helicopters are transitioning to glass cockpits. (US ARMY)

BELOW: New immersive cockpits and helmet sights will improve the situational awareness of future US Army aviators. (BELL TEXTRON)

ABOVE: The MQ-1C 25M is the extended range variant of the Gray Eagle UAV. (GENERAL ATOMICS)

BELOW: General Atomics' Mojave short take-off and landing UAV will allow the US Army to deploy future unmanned systems to improvised landing strips. (GENERAL ATOMICS)

attrition of its aircraft and weapon systems. Although the US Army suffered numerous casualties in Iraq and Afghanistan in a drip, drip, drip of insurgent attacks, these were never on a scale that threatened to make whole companies, battalions or brigades combat non-effective. This new sort of conflict requires a complete change in mindset, tactics and operational procedures.

The potential for a confrontation between the US and China presents the US Army with major challenges and opportunities. At first glance, the Pacific theatre appears to offer little opportunity for US Army forces to play an important role. The USAF and US Navy have dominated the American response to growing Chinese power until now. Air and naval power are seen as the key to protecting important American allies in the Pacific, such as Australia, Japan, the Philippines, South Korea and Taiwan, by keeping sea lanes open and ensuring air supremacy. The idea of the US Army going toe-to-toe with the Chinese People's Liberation Army in a ground war in Asia does not seem sensible.

The US Army still has an important part to play in any military confrontation with China, which will require strong aviation assets, both manned and unmanned. First, the US has a key mission to defend South Korea from its northern neighbour. This will require powerful land and aviation assets to take on North Korea's heavily equipped army. Meanwhile, China is developing strong amphibious forces to strike at strategic islands across the Pacific.

LEFT: The US Army is fielding new technology to defeat enemy UAVs, including anti-drone guns that disrupt their electronic systems, causing them to crash. (US ARMY)

Taiwan, as well as islands belonging to the Philippines and Japan, are all within easy reach of such attacks. US Army ground and aviation forces could play an important role in defending against any Chinese invasions and then launching offensives to throw the invaders back into the sea.

Holding key islands in the Pacific which host strategic air and naval bases is an important mission for the US Army. Defending them against Chinese air and missile attack is also the responsibility of the army, because it controls America's land-based air defences. The service is also fielding a new generation of land-based long-range cruise missile launchers. These islands will require strong US Army forces, including aviation, to defend them.

The geography of the Pacific means that the next generation of US Army helicopters, aircraft and drones will have to have much longer ranges to enable them to operate effectively in the region. The Bell MV-25 Valor FLRAA offers a glimpse of the type of aviation capabilities that America is looking to bring into service to fight in this new strategic environment. The MV-25 should be ready by 2028 to begin replacing the US Army's fleet of Black Hawk assault helicopters.

BELOW: A successor to the AH-64E Apache has yet to be developed to escort future tiltrotors carrying assault troops. (BELL TEXTRON)

ABOVE: The Sikorsky Raider was a contender in the US Army Future Attack Reconnaissance Aircraft project before it was cancelled in February 2024. (LOCKHEED MARTIN/ SIKORSKY)

BELOW: US Army aviators are learning to operate from US Navy warships as part of the Pentagon's shift of emphasis to the Pacific region to counter the rise of Chinese military power. (US ARMY, SPC DARBI COLSON)

This will give the US Army a similar capability to the USAF and US Marine Corps' Bell-Boeing V-22 Osprey tiltrotor.

The old Beechcraft MC/RC-12 and de Havilland Canada (DHC) Dash 7 and 8-based fixed wing surveillance aircraft are also being replaced by a new system based on the Bombardier Global Express executive jet, which gives them far longer range and endurance. The MQ-1C 25M extended range variant of the US Army's main surveillance drone has long-range capability that will come online in the near future.

A major looming challenge for the US Army Aviation Branch is how to replace its stalwart Apache attack helicopters to field a capability that can provide aerial firepower to support the MV-25 on long-range missions. The Future Attack Reconnaissance Aircraft (FARA) project was scrapped in 2024 to divert funding to near-term modernisations of the existing helicopter and drone fleet. However, it will not be long before the US Army has to revisit this issue. Is there room for an armed tiltrotor to fight alongside the V-280 or can this mission be

carried out by an armed drone? The AH-64E is still in production and will probably have another 10 or 15 years of service left. This means work will have to start in the near future on a replacement for the AH-64. Whether the US Army's future aerial firepower is delivered by another helicopter, a tiltrotor or a drone has yet to be decided but, whatever the outcome, it will be a major milestone.

How this fits into Pete Hegseth's future plans for the US Army are still unclear. In April 2025, he unveiled his Army Transformation Initiative to rejig his future spending priorities and plans. There are already hints that he might downsize the US Army's infantry and tank forces to enable resources to be moved to weapons more suitable for a large-scale war against China. Hegseth's first round of decisions included an instruction to field new drone swarms into each US Army combat division by 2026, accelerating the withdrawal of the older AH-64D helicopters and UAVs, such as the RQ-7. Combat aviation brigades are also to be reorganised, including the disbanding of the air cavalry squadron in active duty units, to allow their AH-64Es to be redistributed to other units.

The US Army remains committed to operating in the air. The so-called third dimension of warfare is crucial to victory on land, so America's army will be looking to ensure it remains ahead of its opponents in the skies, as well as on the ground.